Electronic Learning:
From Audiotape
to Videodisc _____

Electronic Learning:
From Audiotape to Videodisc _____

Jerome Johnston
The University of Michigan

 LAWRENCE ERLBAUM ASSOCIATES, PUBLISHERS
1987   Hillsdale, New Jersey   Hove and London

Lawrence Erlbaum Associates, Inc., Publishers
365 Broadway
Hillsdale, New Jersey 07642

Library of Congress Cataloging in Publication Data

Johnston, Jerome.
   Electronic learning, from audiotape to videotape.

   Bibliography: p.
   Includes indexes.
     1. Audio-visual education—United States.   2. Educational technology—United States.   I. Title.
LB1043.J59   1987   371.3'3   87-15424
ISBN 0-8058-0012-3
ISBN 0-8058-0026-3 (pbk.)

Printed in the United States of America
10 9 8 7 6 5 4 3 2 1

*Funds for the writing of the book were
provided by The Corporation for
Public Broadcasting*

Contents _____

Preface _____

This book is an update and expansion of Chu and Schramm's classic work, *Learning from Television—What the Research Says.* In their book, Chu and Schramm summarized hundreds of research studies aimed at answering questions such as: Do pupils learn from television? Under what conditions is learning maximized? How do learners and teachers like using television for learning? The book was first released in 1968 and was based on research available through 1967. A second printing appeared in 1974. In this version, Chu and Schramm's television reviews were unchanged, but Monty Stanford added a chapter reviewing the evidence for effectiveness of radio for instruction. He also added three new generalizations regarding instructional television; these were based on his review of additional research completed between 1967 and 1972. The book was reprinted a third time in 1979, and was identical to the 1974 edition. Essentially, then, Chu and Schramm's conclusions are based on the television and radio research in print as of 1972.

This volume is an update in the sense that it includes research as recent as 1985; it is an expansion in that it considers technology other than television and radio, especially the new microprocessor-based technologies. But it is different from Chu and Schramm in several important ways. First, it begins with a brief survey of human learning and instruction. Technologies are being used both to supplement and substitute for more traditional, nontechnological processes such as classroom teaching and print-based workbooks. The potential uses of technology in instruction can best be judged when the elements of conventional face-to-face instruction without electronic media are appreciated. Second, this book is organized differently. Although proliferation of new information technologies has been very rapid, many of the innovations are not fundamentally new. They represent the repackaging of a few basic electronic media: audio, video, and electronic text and graphics. These three categories are used to organize the review of the research literature. Although the concept of medium is a useful organizer, the perspective expressed in this book is that medium per se accounts for only a small portion of the impact of electronic instruction. The burden of instruction rests not on the medium as much as the programming—the instructional strategies, the content, and the motivational elements (music, entertainment, and pace). The educational potential of both the medium and the programming are influenced by the technology used to deliver them because the technology determines the amount of control a learner has over the delivery of the educational messages.

This book came about in response to the needs of the Corporation for Public Broadcasting to understand current thinking about the role of technology in learning and instruction. In May 1984, the Office of Policy Development and Planning of the Corporation for Public Broadcasting (CPB) circulated a "Research Plan for Evaluating the Educational Uses of Technologies." The purpose of the document was to provide a blueprint for the next 5 years of research into the educational uses of technology. This research would help CPB gain a "comprehensive understanding of both current and potential uses of telecommunication technology to enhance education in America." Such a comprehensive understanding requires examination of a number of factors, such as how learners develop and recognize a need to learn, what media they prefer for learning, what role decision makers (e.g., teachers) play in shaping the media choices of learners and current and future uses of technology throughout society. This book is one component in this comprehensive assessment.

The ideas expressed here are the author's responsibility, but they profited from the input of several people. Ric Grefe and Ted Coltman at CPB saw the importance of this book, and urged its basic organiza-

tion around three media. Richard Clark and Gavriel Salomon provided many insights about the paradigm shift in media research that
occurred since Chu and Schramm completed their work.

Jerome Johnston

Foreword _____

"Can the media teach?" asks Dr. Johnston in the book you are about to read. He answers, "No, but mediated programming can."

Further on he qualifies that answer: "With the right software, hardware, and mindware." "Mindware" is a term coined by Salomon and refers to the mindset a learner brings to media instruction—what he or she expects to learn from the material, how interesting and useful it promises to be. It is refreshing to see a concept similar to that worked into an equation on the effectiveness of media for teaching. It means that the old one-way models of media pouring knowledge into passive learners, the patterns we used to read about in mid-century, are now out of style. Learning, whether mediated or face-to-face, is an active process. The learners must be active. The media must be chosen and programmed for active learning. The context must be conducive to learning.

In the late 1960s Dr. Godwin Chu and I published a book called *Learning from Television—What the Research Says.* In that book we summarized a large number of studies on the use of television for instruction, and in a later edition, Monty Stanford added a chapter on instructional radio. Dr. Johnston is kind enough to call this volume an updating of our volume, although it is obvious that he goes beyond it into later developments in the use of electronic text and videodisc.

What he presents in these pages is an updating of what has been learned recently by trial and research about all the electronic media used for instruction.

His update is worth your attention. Electronic learning is becoming ever more common, to keep up with increasingly complex curricula or changing technology. Therefore, self-study promises to demand more and more from and offer more and more to both students in school and workers at home or in the workplace. The situation for such study has changed greatly. As Johnston says, "Electronic media are all around us. Audio, video, and electronic text and graphics are as much a part of daily life as direct experience was a century ago." An example of what this means to the use of electronic media is the experience of China when, 3 years ago, it started an Open University and within a few weeks received 5 million applications for entrance.

For a quick look at the kind of conclusion that emerges from this study, let me suggest that you read the last sentences of a few chapters, and then go back over the text to see how he arrived at that conclusion. For example:

(Chapter 5) "The research done to date suggests that when the topic is appropriate, when tutorial instruction is called for, and when the cost is justified in terms of the number of people to be trained, videodisc instruction can be made at least as effective as live classroom instruction—perhaps even more effective."

(Chapter 4) "As with video, the success of computer-based instruction rests more with the design of the instructional program than it does with the medium itself."

(Chapter 3) "The selection of audio as a medium for instructional programming, and radio or audiotape as a technology for distribution, is defensible on a number of grounds. The selection needs to be made, however, on the basis of the needs of the learning audience."

Even these brief examples suggest that Dr. Johnston has many provocative and useful things to say.

This is a solid and informed volume that sets out to do a large task, and it will prove useful in bringing more nearly up to date our knowledge of a very important subject.

Wilbur Schramm

Chapter 1 _____

Teaching, Learning, and Media

Today, there is increasing use of electronic media in teaching. This is occurring in response to several trends. One trend is that society is attaching greater value to mastering new bodies of information and new skills. School children must learn not only the basic skills of reading and writing, but also algebra, chemistry, and computer programming. High school graduation requirements are increasing in number, and among the requirements are topics for which some teachers were not trained. Adults who have left traditional school settings are faced with the need to master new bodies of information, or to acquire new skills, in order to obtain or maintain employment in a rapidly changing economy.

A second trend relates to the urgency of meeting these educational needs by non-traditional means. The economic failings of the United States in the early 1980s have been laid partly at the feet of poorly trained students and workers. A number of reports on the state of the nation's schools appeared in the years 1983–1984. These reports called for better educational opportunities than the public schools have been providing in order to meet the global challenge of a qualified work force for the 1990s. Business and industry have been faced with the challenge more immediately. New procedures and processes are necessary to be competitive in the world market, and this means training and retraining workers efficiently. To do this, industry has been faced with the overwhelming task of establishing an educational infrastructure to handle rapid training of employees, because the processes used in business and manufacturing change so frequently. Some estimates place the annual cost of industrial training at the same level as that of higher education—$100 billion.

A third trend is the evolution of information technologies. In a short period, we have witnessed the development of highly sophisticated devices for information exchange and retrieval. Some are capable of responding to the needs of learners as defined by either student or instructor. In recent years, the number and quality of these devices has increased as the cost has declined.

AN AGE-OLD QUESTION: CAN THE MEDIA TEACH?

As new technological capabilities emerge, it is natural to ask what part they can play in solving the educational dilemmas of this decade. Can they provide efficiencies in the educational sector? This question has been asked repeatedly over the last 3 decades, although the terms have been somewhat different. Instead of *technology,* the question has been phrased in terms of *media,* by which authors have meant radio, television, and other audiovisual devices. (The term *media* is discussed more extensively at a later point.) As Schramm (1977) noted:

> During the last few decades we have frittered away an enormous amount of research time asking relatively useless questions about the media of instruction. *Can the media teach?* has been asked over and over again, and over and over again the answer has come back: *of course,* students can learn effectively from the media, from *any* medium. *Can they teach as well as a teacher?* The answer: what they can do, they can do as well as a classroom teacher, sometimes better. It depends on the performance of the teacher, the content of the media, what is being taught, and to whom. *Is one medium any more effective than others?* For some purposes, probably yes, but overall there is no superlative medium of instruction, any more than there is one simple algorithm for selecting one medium over others. We have come to realize in recent decades that learning from the media is not an area that lends itself to simple answers. It is an extremely complex multivariate process that challenges us, if we are to understand it, not to ask the simple questions, but rather to concern ourselves with the conditions

for selecting one medium over another, for combining and for using media. (p. 14)

In coming to this conclusion, Schramm did not have the advantage of more recent research. Some of this research explores new types of media content—for example, "The Electric Company," which combines entertainment with instruction in reading. Other research examines new media such as electronic text and graphics manipulated on new technologies such as a personal microcomputer or a videodisc. This book examines research on the impacts of hundreds of media-based programs and asks under what conditions, for what kinds of learners, and with what content have they proven to be effective vehicles for learning. The book answers some of Schramm's traditional media questions for more media and with more recent research.

Media is Only a Vehicle

To answer these questions, certain terms need to be defined more precisely. First, the term *effective* implies making a judgment relative to a standard. For example, is an electronic medium of instruction effective relative to face-to-face instruction without electronic media— the traditional mode of instruction? This means we must describe the elements of traditional modes of learning and instruction. Second, although it is desirable to frame the question in terms of media, it must be noted that the term *medium* means "an agency, such as a person, object or quality, by means of which something is accomplished, conveyed, or transferred" (American Heritage Dictionary). The electronic media are vehicles through which programming is passed to a learner. We cannot explore the potential of a medium independent of the programming being carried on it. A medium has a potential that may or may not be exploited. Prior to "Sesame Street," televised instruction was very much of the "talking head" variety. "Sesame Street" departed from this formula and married entertainment and instruction. The producers took advantage of the video medium in an entirely different way. What one could say about the potential of the visual medium subsequent to "Sesame Street" is quite different from prior assessments—not because the medium changed, but because producers at Children's Television Workshop discovered a new way to exploit the medium.

Similarly, we cannot ignore how technology has altered the potential of each medium of instruction. The video medium has a certain potential as a vehicle for programming. In its early years, this medium was used only in a linear format, as the technology of open-circuit broadcast was used to transmit the programming. Technology has now made possible distribution of the same video programming on both videotape and videodisc. Both of these forms provide a new potential for video by overcoming the limitation of linear consumption. Programs can now be played over and over again or even edited into segments and adapted to the varied learning needs found within a heterogeneous student population. This new potential interacts with the design of programming. With a broadcast technology, producers had to develop a single unified program that would match the needs and abilities of a diverse audience. Yet, teachers know that even homogeneous groupings of 25 students contain a diversity of student preparation and ability that makes a single presentation inadequate. Aiming for the average student in the class, the teacher invariably decides that some concepts will require additional explanations aimed at students whose preparation is inadequate for the learning goals. Accordingly, the teacher prepares multiple presentations and uses them as needed to insure reasonably uniform learning by the whole class. The videodisc permits this same kind of multiple presentation—a main program with branches suitable for learners who need a different kind of explanation. So, to produce video programming that takes advantage of the videodisc technology is a different task; it entails designing not one, but many interrelated programs.

Considerations such as these guided the structure of this book. In this chapter, a brief overview of learning and instructional theory is presented with an emphasis on where media of all types fit into these processes. This is done to provide perspective on the enormity of the task entailed in packaging effective instruction in a media-based program. The electronic media are further defined and classified into three categories: audio, video, and electronic text and graphics. The relationship between media and technology is elaborated, and programming is classified and related to media. The remainder of the book explores the evidence for the effectiveness of programming made for audio, video, and electronic text and graphics. The strengths and weaknesses of each medium are described. The conditions associated with learning are discussed, including issues of program design, learner characteristics, distribution technology, and context factors.

THE PROCESS OF LEARNING

How do people learn new things? How do they remember new information, develop new insights, acquire attitudes, or develop behavioral skills? These questions have filled the life work of many psychologists, yet there are still no simple answers. In fact, in the past decade psychologists have come to think that the processes of learning are more complex than previously imagined, and that they vary widely among individuals.

From Behavioral to Cognitive Psychology

Up until the late 1970s behavioral psychologists dominated the learning field. Their focus was primarily on simple learning tasks. Extrapolations from their research suggested that relatively simple processes were involved in acquiring new knowledge. Stated simplistically, the dominant view of the behaviorists was that learners are passive, they learn new information in response to a properly structured environment, and teaching is the process of presenting learners with new information and reinforcing them when they produce the correct response. From this view it makes sense to use one-way technologies like radio and television to present learners with new ideas. A properly designed audio or video program can present new information in interesting formats and in appropriate-sized chunks, and do it time after time with the same quality. Reinforcement can come from the pleasure of listening or viewing the program, or from a teacher reinforcing learners for demonstrating that they learned the information in the program.

Although the behaviorists' notions were useful for explaining the acquisition and retention of simple information, they did not explain the development of complex insights and syntheses of information—the goal of much of schooling. Accordingly, cognitive psychologists have been looking at what happens internally as individuals process new information—how they attend to, store, and integrate new ideas with existing knowledge. The current view is that learning is an active, constructive process in which learners utilize metacognitive processes such as planning and setting goals to control attending to certain stimuli, organizing the information, and generating appropriate responses. Cognitive approaches view what the teacher does as less important than what the learner does. A teacher's role is to urge the learner to develop and utilize appropriate learning strategies. This view attributes less value to most mediated presentations—

especially if the audience contains inefficient learners. Although an electronic presentation can play an important role in selecting salient stimuli for the learner, it has limited potential to guide how a learner will process the stimuli. This is not true of all media-technology combinations, as is discussed later. But it does place a different burden on media programs. To be effective, they need to be conceived not only as vehicles for information transmission, but also as mechanisms that can help learners effectively process the very information contained therein.

Although many of the ideas of cognitive psychologists are not fully verified, their views have shaped much of the current thinking about the nature of learning. The implications for teaching are not fully known, but one psychologist, Robert Gagné, has a theory of instruction that fits this more complex view of learning in a way that helps conceptualize the role of teachers and media. But before turning to his theory, consider first the many varieties of learning outcomes sought by learners. This adds another layer of complexity to the problem of understanding how individuals learn, but it is an essential layer.

Learning Outcomes

The array of possible learning outcomes is quite wide. Different outcomes require different processes for learners and therefore different instructional strategies for teachers. Learning to play tennis and learning the history of tennis are quite different learning activities. The former requires the development of both intellectual and motor skills, whereas the latter is essentially an intellectual activity. Based on distinctions in the outcome expected and in the character of instruction required to achieve it, Gagné (1984) suggests that learning outcomes can be classified into five categories:

- *Verbal information.* Bodies of verbal information and their interrelationship. For example, how the stock market works or a history of the United States in the 19th century. Learning of verbal information typically requires memorizing discrete facts, concepts, and principles, and then applying them to make discriminations and inferences.
- *Intellectual skills.* Basic learning skills such as reading, writing, computation, and speech.

- *Cognitive strategies.* Skills by which learners control their internal processes of attending, learning, and remembering.
- *Motor skills.* For example, playing tennis or piano; or exercising social skills such as helping or assertiveness.
- *Attitudes.* Predispositions toward groups, objects, or activities.

Verbal Information.   The name for this category derives from the fact that a learner acquires and displays mastery of verbalizable information. This category includes a wide variety of skills ranging from mastering labels for objects to learning abstract principles that explain how things interrelate. Gagné (1977) distinguishes five types of verbal learning. *Chains* refers to labeling an object, as when a child learns the name for "shoe" or an adult learns the label "videodisc." *Multiple discrimination* describes the activity of distinguishing the correct labels among multiple similar objects, as when a learner, presented with a collection of 10 rocks, places the igneous and metamorphic rocks into separate groupings. *Concepts* are abstract qualities such as color or hardness. *Principles* are the rules that govern the relationship among things; for example, gas expands when heated and contracts when cooled. *Problem solving* refers to a learner using concepts and principles to solve a novel situation or problem.

The process of memorization and recall are simpler learning tasks than understanding and application. Some tasks in the verbal information category require only memorization from the learner; other tasks in the same topic area require the learner to memorize labels and rules and then apply them to novel situations.

Intellectual Skills.   Gagné distinguishes between verbal learning and intellectual skills. Using the same categories as in verbal learning, he points to a child learning the fundamental chains and discriminations, such as letters and numbers, fundamental concepts such as whole numbers and fractions, and principles such as addition. Although these are all classified as verbal information, he argues that the strategies for teaching them are different from teaching verbal information, because the latter depends on a learner having already mastered these basic understandings and skills.

Cognitive Strategies.   These are related to intellectual skills, but the emphasis is on the metacognitive or controlling strategies used to acquire and apply information. The category includes strategies such as scanning, questioning, chunking, and comprehension monitoring.

Motor Skills.   Development of motor skills requires the mastery of some verbal information for accurate production of the skill, but that is seldom sufficient. Executing a proper groundstroke in tennis or playing an arpeggio in music requires a learner to match intellectual information about proper motoric behavior of the body with extensive practice to produce the modeled behavior. A special subcategory of motor skills includes social interaction skills, such as being helpful or being assertive.

Attitudes.   Included here are attitudes toward groups such as minorities and women, or activities such as drinking. The category also includes attitudes toward learning by itself—for example, attitudes toward studying science or practicing and perfecting musical skills.

The first three categories in Gagné's scheme match closely those employed by other cognitive psychologists who distinguish among (a) declarative knowledge, (b) procedural knowledge, and (c) cognitive strategies. Gagné's scheme is a little more useful to those interested in media, because it includes behavioral skills and attitudes—areas for which many media programs have been created in recent years (see Johnston & Ettema, 1986, for a review).

How Learning Occurs

Most learning is the result of an interplay between processes internal to the individual and events external to the individual. When the external events are assembled in ways designed to enhance internal processes in an individual, the events are called *instruction.* The processes internal to the individual have been the focus of long-standing attention by learning theorists in psychology. The most fruitful theory for education is the information-processing model of learning. It postulates that learning is comprised of a number of processes between the point when a learner is stimulated by something that is to be learned and the point when a response is produced that indicates that learning has occurred. Among the processes are attention to the stimulus, selective perception of characteristics of the stimulus, retention in short-term memory, semantic encoding, storage in long-term memory, retrieval of information, response generation, performance, and feedback regarding performance.

A major life work for the individual learner is developing strategies that can make these internal processes efficient. Generally speaking, the strategies are called *metacognitive* or *controlling processes.* For example, effective reading requires a series of complex interactions between the reader and text. The reader may need to skim the reading material first to establish an organizational scheme, use the context to decode unfamiliar words, and summarize the material to check for understanding and remembering. If the reader fails to comprehend some material, he or she may need to employ the strategy of rereading. It is the proper deployment of these strategies that distinguishes good from poor readers. Although there are some learning strategies that are common to all learning activities, current thinking focuses on the different strategies required for mastering material in different subject areas (e.g., math vs. reading).

As psychologists break down abilities into multiple discrete strategies, conceptions of intelligence are evolving. Instead of postulating that there are two relatively stable capacities (verbal and math), current conceptions talk of multiple intelligences and consider that these capabilities can be altered by proper training.

Another construct in the learning paradigm is motivation—the learner's inclination toward effortful strategic behavior. Although there are several competing models that attempt to explain how motivation operates, (attribution models and expectancy-value models), they all contend that individuals will expend effort on a learning task to the extent the task is perceived as having benefit to the individual. Learners will not expend effort on tasks that have little immediate value, or at which the learner thinks he or she cannot be successful.

THE PROCESS OF TEACHING

Most formal learning occurs under the guidance of a teacher in an instructional situation. The teacher is responsible for orchestrating verbal statements, objects, pictures, printed text, and audio-visual materials in a way that will result in the learner acquiring the desired information or skills. The focus in this book is on electronic media and programming designed to teach—to orchestrate electronically all or part of what human teachers do. Before examining the media's record in this regard, it is useful to consider a number of aspects of face-to-face instruction: (a) the events of instruction—ways in which teachers bring the external environment to bear on a learner's internal processes; (b) common modes of instruction; and (c) media—sources of stimulation at the teacher's disposal.

Events and Modes of Instruction

For those interested in the design of instruction, the multi-stage theory of human learning provides a rich array of possibilities. It suggests that effective instruction must involve much more than simply presenting a stimulus to a learner. In this vein, Gagné and Briggs (1974) have identified nine different activities, which they call the events of instruction, that a teacher can use to facilitate learning. Each event is designed to match one of the nine learning processes mentioned earlier. The events are described in Table 1.1. Gagné (1977) argues that all of these events are involved in each act of learning, although not all of them need to be provided by the external events of instruction. Increasingly, as learners move from novice to experienced in a particular knowledge domain, they develop their own resources (metacognitive skills) to provide the necessary guidance for learning.

Depending on the instructional task, teachers select from among six modes of instruction to provide the events of instruction described previously. In a lecture mode the teacher is primarily providing information, although the lecture can be used as well to stimulate students to become interested in the subject or to study more. In a recitation mode, students are provided opportunities to rehearse what they have learned and secure feedback on their performance. The discussion mode is used to provide an opportunity to apply what is being learned and secure clarification about the material. The laboratory mode is also suitable for learning that entails observation and analysis of phenomena. The tutoring mode is used to provide one-on-one help in acquiring the information or skill desired. Finally, the homework mode is designed to provide independent opportunity to read, memorize, and engage in activities the teacher judges important to attaining the outcomes of the course. Teachers choose one or more modes based on the goals of the course and the learning needs of their students. The more diverse the group of students, the more complicated is a teacher's strategy of selection.

The Sources of Learning: Direct vs. Mediated Experience

A teacher uses a variety of stimuli in the process of instruction. Some stimuli represent direct experience for the learner, others indirect or mediated experience. A teacher can give a learner direct experience with the objects of instruction. For the kindergartener it might be the

TABLE 1.1
The Events of Instruction

1. *Gaining attention.* A stimulus is presented to appeal to the learner's interest or curiosity. It may be a question, a challenge, a demonstration, a sharp change in the visual scene, or the like.

2. *Informing the learner of the objective.* The learner needs to know how she or he will know when the performance objective of the lesson has been achieved.

3. *Stimulating recall of prerequisite learned capabilities.* For any except the most fundamental learning, the learner must have at hand certain knowledge and skills previously learned in order to apply them in the new task.

4. *Presenting the stimulus material.* When the learner is ready, the material to be learned must be presented.

5. *Providing "learning guidance."* The learner needs to be directed by prompts, hints, or questions toward the objective.

6. *Eliciting the performance.* Having arrived at the objective, the learner must now be challenged to show that she or he can "do it," perhaps by use of an example or problem.

7. *Providing feedback.* The learner must be informed of the correctness of his or her performance—by words, by a smile or a nod, or by some other means.

8. *Assessing performance.* The teacher wants to make sure that the learner has accomplished the objective.

9. *Enhancing retention and transfer.* This calls for practice, especially with varied tasks requiring the same skill that has been the objective of the lesson.

NOTE: After Gagné and Briggs, 1974, p. 123ff. and Schramm, 1977: p. 74.

actual objects to be counted; for the high school student it might be the chemicals to be mixed to learn about compounds and mixtures. When a teacher wants to illustrate something about objects or processes, he or she can perform a demonstration using the actual objects and communicate orally the points he or she wishes to make. Direct experience is important and even essential to some learning tasks. Very young learners need to manipulate objects before they learn abstract notions such as names or how to count objects. At the other extreme, many industrial trainers feel that instruction about the use of machines or processes also requires direct hands-on experience.

Most of what is called *formal instruction,* however, does not use direct experience; it heavily depends on mediated experience. Because it is too difficult or expensive in many cases to have actual objects under study in the classroom, a teacher often selects a visual medium to represent the objects, either photographs or figures. When a still photo or drawing is inadequate because of the dynamic nature of the process, a motion picture can be used to capture the sequence of events.

The most extensively used mediated experience is printed text. One type of text is itself the object of learning; for example, a novel or historical document. It is examined by students to ascertain its meaning or to consider the value of its message. Another type is a textbook specifically designed for instruction. It may include portions of primary text, but the essential component is a wraparound of explanatory material that represents instruction about the primary material.

Three more media are called electronic because storage and transmission of information in these media is done electronically. These are the media of audio, video, and electronic text and graphics.

This brief overview highlights the complexity of the teaching process and, therefore, the enormity of the task facing those who would design instructional programming for any of the electronic media. The obvious strengths of electronic instruction are in those events and modes that can be accomplished with one-directional presentations: attracting the attention of the learner, presenting the objectives of the lesson, reminding the learner of prerequisite skills and information, and presenting new stimulus material. But these are only four of the nine events. The other events involve guiding, tutoring, and assessing students along the way—events that require evaluation of individual student attainments. It is the complexity of the teaching process that explains why so much of the instructional material available for the electronic media is supplementary, designed not to supplant but to enhance one or more instructional events, while the overall process of instruction remains under the control of a human teacher.

ELECTRONIC MEDIA, TECHNOLOGY, AND PROGRAMMING

For each of the electronic media there are a number of questions that can be usefully asked. What characterizes and distinguishes the medium, what kind of instructional content can the medium carry, and how does the technology that delivers a particular mediated program affect its potential to teach? As subsequent chapters of this book show, there is evidence that well-designed programs suitable to the medium, utilizing the appropriate technology, can do a very effective job of teaching. Usually, learners require additional input in the form of textbooks and face-to-face instruction by a teacher; occasionally a program is self sufficient and can stand alone. But in most cases, the issue is not whether the medium is capable of delivering instruction; rather, what are the strengths of the medium and a particular delivery technology for presenting a particular type of learning task to learners with certain needs and characteristics.

Electronic Media

This book distinguishes among three primary electronic media: audio, video, and electronic text and graphics. The chapters are organized around these distinctions. These categories are useful, because they correspond to the historical development of electronic media for instructional purposes. Audio was first used with radio and then audiotape. Video, which combined aural and visual elements, gave rise to instructional television. Then came electronic text and graphics— a phrase that describes the essential components of computers. The computer technology itself, however, has made it possible to combine the several media, so it is useful to think of a fourth category—hybrid media. An example is the integrated videodisc that combines all three media in a single package. Advancements in electronics will result in further melding of the media, as digitized sound (voice, music, etc.) and digitized visuals give to computers all of the instructional capabilities formerly kept quite distinct. However, because the three basic media serve different (albeit, overlapping) instructional purposes, they need to be considered separately. What characterizes these media and distinguishes them one from the other? This is a complex question, tied to the ways humans communicate and use symbols. The issue is discussed at length elsewhere (e.g., Arnheim, 1974; Salomon, 1979), and further discussion can be found in the later chapters of this book. Here are some general notions about each medium and its unique instructional potential.

Audio.   By itself, audio is used in instruction in a variety of forms. Most notable are radio, audiotape, and records. Audio is suitable for music, language instruction, oral discourse (lecture, commentary, etc.), and dramatic presentations enhanced with various sound effects. When it carries discourse it has the advantage of being able to establish a relationship with the listener based on oratory, sonority, and persuasive argument. When the purpose is to persuade, and a particular speaker has the power to evoke, then this medium is ideal. Although audio lacks a visual channel it has a limited capacity to draw on the listener's storehouse of visual images through the cueing possibilities of voices and appropriate sound effects.

Compared to printed text, audio is a slow medium for the transmission of information. Depending as it does on the natural speed of the human voice, audio conveys information much more slowly than can be processed by a learner in a text-literate society. When used with most technologies, audio is a linear medium, requiring the listener to follow the audio track as it was developed by the producer. In contrast, much of learning from experience and from text is non-linear; learners skip some material and review other material to match their personal style of learning. The limitations of linearity can be overcome to some extent with certain technologies. Audio on radio is strictly linear, but using an audiotape recording of the same program permits a listener to replay it and partially compensate for the linearity. This can be useful to some learners, but it is still not as useful as the more random access allowed by printed text and by live presentations in which a listener can ask questions and induce the presenter to elaborate and clarify the original presentation. The type of access—linear or random—is not a function of just the medium or the technology, it is a function of the programming too. The script for a 30-minute radio show is written with the conventions of a linear oral presentation in mind. In such a short time period a very limited argument can be developed. A half-hour live lecture is similarly limited, but the speaker can interrupt the linear flow and branch into related areas if it appears useful to meet the needs of the listeners.

Video.   Video includes pictures and symbols in either a still or motion format. Pictures can show exactly what an object looks like at any given moment; they can show the object over time should motion and change be salient for learning. In many learning areas the visual dimension is essential to comprehension. In chemistry, a visible change occurs in a substance as heat is applied. In sociology, group members display different reactions toward one another depending on the nature of the task and the reward structure for successful task performance. These reactions can be captured visually. In both cases, viewing the events is important to learning, but insufficient without the addition of some form of oral communication in which the events are interpreted. The simplest way to add oral communication is with synchronized audio to accompany the video.

Creating instructional materials in video is a complex task, partly because of the very nature of the medium. Pictures are iconic forms of information, densely packed but ambiguous in their interpretation. Images mean different things depending on a viewers' prior experience and the context at the time it is encoded in memory. As Arnheim (1974) notes, the real event is tied to a time and place and to emotional responses that cannot be created for an individual. Standing at the base of the World Trade Center in New York, all observers would probably discern that they were viewing a very tall building. But the image is personalized for each viewer as she or he notes the size of the nearby pedestrians and compares this with the building by scanning back-and-forth between them and the vertical view up the side of the building. The image to be encoded may be further affected by seeing the building sway in the wind and hearing and feeling gusts of wind swirl around the structure. Winter snow or summer heat can affect the image, as can other human events occurring in the vicinity. When a producer chooses a perspective and records it on video, it represents one particular interpretation of a reality. This can be an advantage or a disadvantage, depending on the instructional purpose of the program. Using a television series on Vietnam to provide a particular perspective on the war may be exactly what is needed to expose young learners to a view and feeling for the war they could not easily acquire without living through that era, and perhaps even fighting in the war. On the other hand, using a videodisc simulation of a chemistry lab titration experiment in place of a live wet lab experience might be inappropriate for learners who do not have sufficient personal experience with manipulating chemicals in a real laboratory.

These considerations speak only to the presentational aspect of the video medium—to the perspective captured in the stimulus material. Salomon (1979) argues that conventions used by videographers in the production of television (e.g., cuts and zooms) can go beyond this and actually cultivate cognitive operations in viewers that enhance their own processing skills. This has yet to be proved, however.

Electronic Text and Graphics.   In one sense, electronic text and graphics is identical to printed text and graphics. As a medium for learning, it has no advantage over printed text until coupled with a microprocessor technology that allows the text to be arranged for the learner in ways that match the learner's needs. No other medium can be orchestrated as easily for presentation of material or for testing learner comprehension. In an application of electronic text and graphics called a *simulation,* the medium has the potential to be used to enhance problem-solving skills in specific content domains. In another application, the medium can be used to present activities that help learners construct their own meaning and sense out of information. Theoretically, the electronic text and graphics medium might be used to cultivate specific metacognitive skills that the cognitive psychologists argue are at the heart of learning. This idea is developed by Patterson and Smith (1986).

TECHNOLOGY

The basic character of each electronic medium varies with the technology used to distribute it. The same audio program can be disseminated on broadcast radio as well as on audio cassette designed for personal tape recorders. The choice of technology can be a mix of strategic, economic, and instructional considerations. Strategically, broadcast radio is suitable for reaching a large audience at a single time. Audio cassettes are suitable for small specialized audiences, and for groups with varying schedules. The same is true for video. Motion pictures—the essence of video—can be distributed with a 16mm projector, broadcast television, Instructional Television Fixed Service (ITFS), cable television, videocassette, or videodisc. Open-circuit broadcast, ITFS, or cable are appropriate technologies for distributing to large audiences at fixed times, whereas film, video-cassette, and videodisc are options for distributing to audiences that have conflicting schedules. The medium is identical; the choice of technology is a strategic or managerial one.

The choice of a technology can also be influenced by instructional concerns. Technologies vary in the amount of control they permit the learner. For a less able learner, or even able learners with little prior background on a topic, the ability to replay a program (i.e., to control the presentation) is an important ingredient in learning. This is illustrated in a study by Gay (1986). In an introductory biology course he divided the class into two groups of the same average aptitude, but differing in their conceptual understanding of protein synthesis. Instruction on this topic was presented using an interactive videodisc. In one condition, however, students had the instruction controlled by the computer, while in another learners could control the sequence, pace, presentation mode, and amount of practice. Those students who had exhibited little prior understanding of protein synthesis did best on a posttest of understanding if their instruction had been controlled by the computer. Conversely, those who had shown significant prior knowledge of protein synthesis did much better when the presentation was under their own control; they spent less time with the videodisc program and achieved as well as students with high prior knowledge who had received their instruction in the computer-controlled condition.

A useful classification of media and technologies was developed by the Corporation for Public Broadcasting (Corporation, 1984). It contains three categories of technology for each medium. *Passive linear technologies* are those in which the user has no control over reception except in a binary sense—receive or not receive. Broadcast radio or television are examples of passive linear technologies. *Interactive communication technologies* provide the user with the possibility of exchanging oral or video information with other users electronically. Telephone is a prime example of this technology. A third type of technology is called *interactive user command and control.* Here the technology gives to the user a command over whatever is stored in the medium, whether it be information or processes. Computer-assisted instruction is the prototypical example. Additional examples are provided in Table 1.2.

The focus of this book is on applications in the categories of passive linear and interactive user command and control. Interactive communication (for example, teleconferencing or computer conferencing) has a place in learning, but there are very few examples where interactive communication technology is used to carry the major burden of instruction. The most common use of interactive communication is to enhance instruction that is conducted primarily using other media, as when a professor can be reached by phone or electronic mail to discuss an issue in a course. There are some examples of using a computer conference to link together students and teachers in a way that extends classroom discussion. These are discussed in chapter 4.

TABLE 1.2
CPB Classification of Information Media and Technologies

Type of Technology	Sample Technology
Audio	
Passive linear	broadcast radio, phono records, audio cassette; telelectures (phone)
Interactive communication	telephone, audio conferencing
Interactive user command and control	language labs, Speak-and-Spell
Video	
Passive linear	broadcast TV, linear videodisc, videotape
Interactive communication	video teleconferencing
Interactive user command and control	interactive videodisc
Electronic Text and Graphics	
Passive linear	teletext
Interactive communication	electronic mail, computer conferencing
Interactive user command and control	computer-assisted instruction, videotex

NOTE: After Corporation for Public Broadcasting, 1984, p. 35.

WHICH MEDIUM FOR WHICH TASK?

To appreciate the relative utility of the different combinations of electronic media and technology, it is useful to consider Carroll's (1974) advice. Although he wrote it more than 10 years ago, and the ideas precede many of the more promising developments in electronic text and graphics, it is still applicable. Carroll believes that print is absolutely essential for the transmission of many ideas. The elaboration of a complex sequence of reasoning with concomitant definitions, qualifications, and logical constraints can be done only with text. Given this as a unique strength of print, Carroll (1974) offers five principles for choosing a medium to meet an educational need:

1. Facts and information that have already been amassed and, perhaps, well analyzed by others are most efficiently learned from

print, to the extent that it is at all necessary to learn them. What the learner needs most, usually, is direct experience in finding and locating information so that he will know where to find new information.

2. For learning that involves understanding of complex concepts and relationships the print mode is often to be favored, for it lends itself to the careful study that may be necessary to acquire understanding. But text should be supplemented by illustrations, diagrams, schematics, etc., wherever appropriate, and the theoretical learning should be alternated with practical experience.

3. If the learning objective entails primarily skill in dealing with persons or things, then demonstrations, concrete experience with the activity, and oral coaching and guidance would seem to be more effective media than print.

4. If the learning objective involves acquiring some kind of direct experience with concrete reality, one should consider how difficult, time-consuming, or expensive it would be to acquire such experience. One should consider the possibilities of giving this experience vicariously through films or other audiovisual aids, or even through print.

5. Many kinds of learning—in particular those that involve the learning of algorithms and procedures, the understanding of hierarchically structured conceptual systems, and practice in applying these algorithms and systems—require active guidance of the learner and reinforcement of and feedback from his responses . . . Ordinarily, printed materials have limited capability of providing such feedback. Most audiovisual media, in fact, share these limitations with print. Nevertheless, print offers considerable possibilities for providing guidance and feedback. Various programmed instruction formats require active response from the learner and give knowledge of results only after the response has been made . . . Unfortunately, printed materials are not always organized in such a way as to provide for feedback and review . . . If active structuring of learning by the medium of instruction is a chief requirement, I suspect that the medium of choice would be CAI (computer-aided instruction), in which it is possible to make the development and pacing of the program depend upon the students' responses. (pp. 177–179)

As these recommendations suggest, the choice of the best medium and technology for a particular instructional task is not a science. It rests with experienced teachers who appreciate the great variety of learning needs in their students and the potential of different mediated presentations to meet those needs. This potential, however, must be assessed knowing the expectations of the learners regarding mediated instruction.

MINDWARE: INTERACTION AMONG MEDIA, EXPECTATIONS, AND CONTEXT

Learning is an active process within an individual requiring that the learner willfully engage the material. Learners differ in their intellectual curiosity—their innate desire to engage new material—and in their skills at decoding messages from various media. Learners also vary in the associations they make with different media. Some associate the media of audio and video with entertainment, not active engagement for learning. Ksobiech (1976) demonstrated how a learner's perception of a task radically affects what is learned from mediated instruction. He showed the same video lesson to three different groups of college undergraduates, but he gave different instructions to each group. One was told to simply evaluate the lesson as a piece of instruction, another was told that they would be tested on the content, and the third was told that they would find the video entertaining, but they would not be responsible for the material. On a subsequent test of content mastery the three groups performed quite differently. The group expecting to be tested performed best, the group evaluating the materials was next best, and the group expecting to be entertained exhibited the poorest performance on the exam. Expectations of the learners regarding how the mediated program should be used affected how they attended to the presentation. It also affected how they sought additional information. Some students in Ksobiech's experiment were allowed to push a button and receive more video or more narrative. The group expecting a test consistently chose more narrative, presumably because they believed it contained the factual information they would need to succeed at the test. This research shows how a learner's expectations alters the potential of the programming. But it also indicates that the perception can be manipulated.

Drawing on a computer metaphor, Salomon (1985) called the learner's propensities and associations with media *mindware*, (to distinguish it from the terms *hardware* and *software*). As can be seen, the learner's mindware greatly affects what he or she will derive from educational programming. In classroom-learning situations, a teacher can alter learners' expectations regarding engagement for learning. This can be done in many ways. Ksobiech used a simple statement by the teacher, but there are other aspects of the context that can affect expectations. Among these are the timing of the presentation, the activities that precede and follow it, and the expectations communicated by fellow students. The point to be made is that a medium and its programming cannot be characterized in a vacuum. Electronic learning is the result of an interaction among media, programming, learner characteristics, and the context or setting in which the electronic instruction is being used.

Instruction is a complex act; human teachers can be responsive to a wide range of needs in a class of students. Teacher judgments are made on the basis of reading subtle cues in learners. A furled brow or a distracted look tell the teacher to change the pace or shift the presentation to stimulate attention or enhance comprehension. By and large, media and the related technology lack this ability to respond to needs of learners in so many different ways. However, when portions of instruction can be codified, and essential sequences of instruction specified, mediated programming can repeat it with the same quality time after time. The lure of most media projects, especially those that involve the electronic media, is the promise of capturing the best of instruction—the stimulating call to learn, the lucid explanation, the vivid portrayal of a complicated phenomenon, the analysis and remediation of learning errors—for repeated use or for use with large numbers of learners.

PROGRAM CHARACTERISTICS

Modest progress has been made in identifying principles to guide the design of effective educational television programs (see summaries by Johnston & Ettema, 1986; Kozma, 1986). In computer-assisted instruction, instructional designers have focused attention on how to present conceptual information (e.g., the work of Tennyson, Reigeluth, or Merrill). But very few studies of the impact of mediated instruction have taken apart the programming under study to identify the essential elements responsible for the measured effects. For this reason, little can be said in this book about the dimensions of programming that account for the reported results. A few distinctions can be made that have an obvious relationship to outcomes:

Subject matter and grade level: For example fourth-grade fractions, or college-level biology.

Breadth and Length: How much material is the program trying to cover? Is it a single unit on the earthworm or is it a multiple-part program covering all invertebrates?

Instructional Sufficiency: To what degree does the program instruct as opposed to simply present new information?

A review of programs in almost any medium suggests three categories of instructional sufficiency: (a) demonstrations, (b) partially sufficient, and (c) stand-alone or automated programs. These categories arise from considering Gagné's instructional events. The demonstration category includes programs designed to extend the primary sources of learning available to a learner. A demonstration presents stimulus material that would be difficult to bring to the classroom, but it does not attempt to perform the instructional tasks of alerting the learner, presenting the learning objectives, reminding the learner of prior information necessary to understand the new concepts, testing for mastery, and so on. An example is a film clip that illustrates what can be seen through an electron microscope—a laboratory device too expensive to bring to the classroom. Another example is an audio recording of a city council meeting or congressional debate which would be impractical for learners to attend first-hand. It is expected that a teacher (or even the student) will provide all of the other instructional support required for learning.

Partially sufficient programming carries some, but not all, of the burden of instruction; a teacher is still needed. Programs in this category vary in the instructional events they provide to the learner. A drill-and-practice computer program may provide a check on mastery by utilizing two of the events: eliciting performance and providing feedback. A tutorial computer program may alert the learner and present new stimulus material as well as check for mastery. Many instructional television programs provide several of Gagné's presentational events (e.g., gaining attention, informing the learner of the objective, stimulating recall of prerequisite learned capabilities, and presenting the stimulus material), but leave the remaining instructional guidance activities to the teacher. A useful example that illustrates the distinction is "Trade-Offs," an upper elementary school economics curriculum from the Agency for Instructional Technology (formerly, the Agency for Instructional Television). The fifteen videotapes, which run 20 minutes, provide the stimulus material for an entire curriculum, and the teacher manual provides guidance to the teacher for all of the instructional events needed to help students learn the material. In their submission to the Joint Dissemination Review Panel the developers note (Agency for Instructional Television, no date):

> The guide materials for each lesson include a statement of content that identifies key concepts, a suggested statement for introducing the program to students, questions and activities to help students resolve the problem posed at the end of the lesson, and other activities for reinforcement or application. To further assist the teacher, the objectives to be accomplished through each program are listed in the guide. The guide was designed to provide maximum help without being restrictive. Most of the suggested teaching techniques are highly flexible.

The Agency argues that this is precisely what is needed these days in many content areas, of which economics is an example.

> Teachers of the elementary curriculum are not, by and large, oriented to teaching economics as part of the elementary curriculum . . . In an [era] characterized by an "information explosion" alternative methods of providing content are sorely needed. (p. 9)

A third category is self-sufficient instruction. This refers to programs designed to be complete in themselves, requiring little or no mediation by a teacher. A good example is the Florida integrated videodisc training program for Aid to Families with Dependent Children (AFDC) workers (chapter 5). All of the instructional components are contained in the videodisc and computer programs, including assessing mastery and providing feedback on performance. Some media and associated technologies permit greater degrees of self-sufficiency than others.

JUDGING THE IMPACT OF
ELECTRONIC INSTRUCTION

What are appropriate criteria to use in judging the utility of electronic instruction? The answer is complex because of the variety of expectations people hold for it. The possibilities can be grouped into a number of categories.

Changes in Learners

The most common measure used in studies of mediated instruction is learner achievement. In the case of programs that teach verbal information or intellectual skills, the question is: can the learner who has been exposed to the instruction demonstrate mastery of the concepts? In the case of a manual or motor skill, can the learner perform it? The evaluations of the early versions of "Sesame Street" asked if children who watched it learned the alphabet and the numbers from 1 to 10.

Attitudes represent people's disposition toward objects and activities. Television is frequently chosen as a medium to influence dispositions about learning. The television series "3-2-1 Contact" was created to demonstrate to girls and minorities the inherent attractiveness of science as an area of study. It was hoped that viewers would subsequently take more interest in scientific inquiry appropriate to their age. In this case, the content of the media program was designed to influence attitudes.

In some cases instruction is developed for an electronic medium with the hope that students will find the electronic version more interesting and motivating than live classroom instruction. As a result, they should persist longer at the learning task. Evaluators of computer-based instruction frequently ask how students like learning via computers. Attitudes toward learning are assessed in two ways. One is to ask learners a variety of satisfaction questions. Another is to monitor course completion; this is often used in assessing various forms of distant learning, such as telecourses.

Changes in learners, once measured, can be judged against an absolute or relative criterion. An absolute criterion is established without using another form of instruction as a referent. This was done in studies of "Sesame Street" which compared viewers with non-viewers. A relative criterion compares mastery of the same material using instruction in two different media. Advocates of media-based instruction often desire to compare mediated instruction with "stand-up" or live classroom instruction. Although desirable from a policy perspective, this type of comparison is not easy to make. It is very difficult to establish "equivalent" instruction where the only difference between the two is the technology. Inevitably, a course is designed and delivered differently in the two forms.

When a comparison is made, it typically entails examining the average pre- to post-achievement scores of the media- and live-instruction groups to see if the gains of one group are different than the other. It is important to look beyond average effects of two programs of instruction, because the benefits may accrue to only a certain subgroup. For example, the Open University in Britain creates curriculum materials for their telecourses in several media, including print, radio, and television. They have found that the radio materials are of greatest value for the academically weak students for whom printed text is difficult to master. The contribution of audio to this subgroup of students would not be revealed in an analysis of the average gains for a heterogeneous group of students.

In the study of computer-based tutorial instruction the comparison of average differences between computer and live instruction is also insufficient. An important claim of most tutorial modes is that individualizing instruction will result in reducing the range of achievement found in group-based instruction. The notion here is that a classroom represents a collection of students with varying ability to comprehend and master the material under study. In the course of any lesson some students understand the material and progress at the pace set by the teacher. Other students fall behind because they do not understand the material. At the end of a unit of instruction, a classroom of students will be characterized by a range of grades on a test of achievement. Proponents of individualizing instruction hope to reduce this variance in outcomes because the approach, in essence, provides tutorial assistance whenever a learner has difficulty understanding the material. For tutorial instruction it is necessary to look both at the mean scores of students and the variance.

Efficiency

Those interested in efficiency of different forms of instruction ask about speed as well as the amount of learning. Here the question is how long does it take students to master the material using different media? The question is raised most often with regard to computer-based instruction designed to act as stand-alone instruction for an entire unit of material. As an example, the Florida Department of Health must train intake workers to determine the eligibility of clients for benefits under a program for AFDC. The conventional classroom course takes 160 hours to complete. In an experiment, the department developed an integrated videodisc program covering the same topic. A key question in the evaluation was whether workers could be trained with the videodisc program in a shorter period of time than conventional classroom instruction. (The answer can be found in chapter 5.)

Efficiency is purchased at a price. It is only one more step to ask the cost–benefit question: if instruction is available in several forms, which form is most cost-beneficial? The answer is not arrived at simply, however. Although it is relatively easy to tally costs of developing and delivering a specific program, the benefits are less easily quantified. Consider offering a college course by radio. How does one quantify the benefit of having the course available in this form if the same course is available in most local community colleges or state universities in the area?

Classroom Management

When an electronic medium is introduced into the classroom it can have varying effects on student response to classroom tasks, and these effects can be part of the judgment of a medium's value. The appearance of a television set may signal a break from the regular routine and garner the attention of students. If students can learn equally well from a televised program on a subject, it may be worth alternating it with live instruction if it can help maintain the interest of students over the course of a lengthy school day. Similarly, if a computer-based drill-and-practice program does as good a job as dittoed work sheets and quizzes, the computer-based teaching may be preferred if a teacher needs it to facilitate the management of a particular group of students. These examples illustrate other aspects of electronic instruction that might be used to justify choosing it over other forms.

Curricular Priorities

The agenda-setting role of mass media programs is well established. Therefore, it can be argued that the presence of widely viewed educational programming could influence what teachers and students consider to be the most important goals in education. In the early 1970s the daily broadcasts of "The Electric Company" had the potential of signaling to parents and youngsters the importance of reading in general, as well as the importance of developing specific skills to improve reading.

Any curricular materials—textbooks or television programs—can alter the way in which subjects are taught. If a compelling case can be made for teaching a subject in a way that differs from common practice, then a media-based program might be in order. In the early 1970s, new approaches were emerging in the field of reading instruction. These were incorporated into "The Electric Company," which in turn was promoted for use in inner-city classrooms where the teachers frequently had not been trained in these methods for teaching the subject. For teachers, "The Electric Company" provided a model of this new approach to reading instruction that they could see (and adopt) as they watched the programs along with their students.

Most of the research studies of electronic learning focus on the impact of a single audio, video, or computer program. Typically, any one study does not assess the program on more than one of these criteria. But collectively the studies allow us to consider the contribution of mediated programming on all these dimensions.

Chapter 2 _____

Audio: Radio, Audiotape, and Telephone

The aural—that which is perceived by the ear—plays a very important role in human life. Music of all kinds enriches human living. The sounds associated with movements and events are essential signals about the character of the environment, whether it is friendly or hostile. The human voice provides information ranging from abstract notions about politics or science to simple utterances about human need ("I'm hungry"). Unlike the printed word, the human voice conveys important affective qualities that tell listeners how to interpret and respond to the information contained in the words.

The term *audio* refers to the electronic transmission of aural material, in both live and recorded forms. The audio medium is utilized in a number of technologies, including telephone, radio, audiotape, and records. More recently, the development of synthesized and digitized speech has given additional meaning to the concept. In this chapter the focus is on audio as a stand-alone medium; in the next chapter it is viewed as an integral part of video.

Audio is the oldest of the media considered in this book. The audio technologies of telephone and phonograph record are both about 100 years old; commercial radio dates back about 60 years. Radio was exploited for educational purposes in the 1930s and the telephone began to be used on a smaller scale in the 1940s (Rao,

1977). As audiotapes and portable recorders improved in quality they too became important tools in education, both for recorded lectures and language instruction. The 1950s and 1960s saw the development of extensive educational programs using all forms of audio. This was especially true in less developed countries. In the 1970s and 1980s television and computers emerged as the glamorous educational media, and stand-alone audio has taken a back seat. In a recent survey of information technology in American education (Office of Technology Assessment, 1982), radio was not identified as a separable technology; audio was either ignored or considered to be an ancillary component of the visual and electronic text media.

Although ignored by some, audio is still an integral part of some large-scale educational efforts. In the early 1970s Britain's Open University was established as a center for "distant learning." The faculty has developed more than 3,000 radio programs and audiotapes for their correspondence courses. Because of its cost-effectiveness alone, audio is an attractive tool in most multi-media instructional efforts.

INSTRUCTIONAL EFFECTIVENESS OF AUDIO

To test the instructional effectiveness of audio, a number of courses originally implemented as face-to-face instruction have been packaged in audio formats on radio or audiotape; less frequently they have been transmitted over the telephone. The audio versions have been tested against their live versions for equivalent "effects."

Radio and Audiotape

There is ample evidence that radio and audiotape—when they duplicate live oral instruction—are as effective as face-to-face instruction. This is true in elementary science (Constantine, 1964), elementary English and music (Wisconsin Research Project in School Broadcasting, 1942; NHK, 1956), high school language instruction (Lumley, 1933; Cook, 1964), and college psychology (Heron & Ziebarth, 1946). In these studies, face-to-face lectures were compared with radio broadcasts of the same content. Typically, it was found that performance of the students exposed to the different media was equivalent; in some instances the radio group was superior. In the Wisconsin study the music students taught by radio did better in recognizing note values, reading at sight, and recognizing rhythms. In one language class

Lumley (1933) reported that the pronunciation of students who had learned by radio was superior. These studies suggest that audio by itself may have an advantage for aural content such as music and foreign language instruction because it forces students to focus solely on the aural components. In a study by Cook (1964), all students in a Spanish class were given classroom instruction. Half of them were given an AM radio over which they could hear regularly scheduled drills in Spanish vocabulary outside of class time. The radio students performed much better on tests. But it is not clear that this was attributable to audio per se, as opposed to simply a greater amount of instructional time; the controls received no instruction outside of class. The novelty of having a radio that could legitimately be used for school work was probably a great motivational tool as well, leading many students to take advantage of the opportunity afforded by the radio.

Research on audiotape is also illuminating. Here too the typical research design begins with an already-existing face-to-face class, and the lectures are recorded on tape. An experimental group uses only the taped lectures whereas the controls have live lectures. Popham (1961) taught a graduate course in Education. He divided the class, carefully matching experimental and control subjects. The experimentals listened to lectures only on tape; the controls attended the live lectures. Those who were taught by the tapes performed equally well on all tests. Menne, Klingenschmidt, and Nord (1969) found the same results for a university psychology course. Given a choice, 209 students chose to use tapes of the lectures, whereas 408 chose the live lectures. Overall, there was no significant difference in test performance.

However, this and one other study show that a taped course can be particularly helpful to certain subgroups of students. In the Menne et al. (1969) study: of all the students (in both live and taped version) who were in the lowest quartile on the pretest, the students using the tapes outperformed the live lecture students. Additionally, only 2.5% of the tape students dropped the course, whereas 15% of the others did. Clearly, self-selection is at work here, but the study suggests an advantage of audiotape for the lower ability students. Similarly, Elliott (1948), in a high school geography course, found that lower IQ students gained relatively more from tape.

This notion of individual differences and benefits of a medium or technology is an important one. The most experienced group in the use of radio for instruction is the British Open University. Most of their courses are multi-media (i.e., there are course components in printed text, television, radio, and audiotape). Bates (1983) reports that student use of radio is extremely varied and the benefits accrue to a certain group:

> Some students listen to none [of the radio programs], others listen to them all. Some listen to half . . . Although radio may not be used a great deal by a lot of students, those students who do use it regularly find it extremely valuable . . . The *weaker* students who do watch or listen rate the broadcasts as *more* helpful than do the more successful students.

Quoting another Open University researcher, Bates continues:

> It is possible that broadcasts in many courses are genuinely more helpful for weak students than for more successful students. Since weak students tend to find the correspondence texts difficult and less helpful (than strong students), these students would seem to need more help from other components. (pp. 73–74 passim)

These studies suggest the limitation of looking for gross learning differences between live and mediated instruction. At least with audio, it has been found that one medium may be superior to another for only certain students.

Telephone

For a long time, the telephone has been used as a technology for extending the aural beyond the classroom. So-called teleteaching became popular in the 1950s as a way to extend the classroom in the same way as radio, but was used for groups too small or specialized to justify open-circuit radio broadcasts. The primary use has been to bring lectures—called *telelectures*—to remote groups. In 1947, in an attempt to provide post-graduate dentistry education between the University of Illinois and 30 dentists in Scranton, PA, this teleteaching method was used. There were six 2-hour lectures, each followed by a live question-and-answer period—something not possible with one-way audio technologies.

Psychology students at the University of Omaha had a discussion with Neil Miller, the author of their text, at Yale University. The technology allowed the students to have personal contact with the author supposedly with the effect of motivating their subsequent pursuit of the subject.

To improve science teaching at a number of widely separated colleges, thirteen 45-minute lectures were transmitted to each campus using an amplified telephone. Each lecture was given by an expert and was followed by a question and answer period. It is not known how much was learned by this technique, but its unique value may have been motivational. One participant commented: "It is highly unlikely that any students or teachers would have an opportunity to discuss person-to-person the major ideas of such a distinguished company" (Rao, 1977, p. 475).

Rao (1977) summarizes the scant research on instructional effectiveness: "Though somewhat limited in scope, the research done on effectiveness of teleteaching indicates that teleteaching is an economical and effective tool" (p. 483).

Rao notes that a number of advances have extended the possibilities of teleteaching. These include ways to couple graphics using a device called the *electrowriter*. These technologies have been replaced today by networked computers with writing tablet input and multicolor graphic output (see chapter 5).

One other use can be noted. For a long time, the telephone has been used for the homebound or hospitalized student. In this system, a teacher (either a normal classroom teacher or a special teacher for the homebound group) has a console that can be used to automatically dial up students. Individual instruction can be carried on between teachers and students or in a group using a conference call feature. Rao (1977) summarizes the scant research on this application and reports that it was uniquely useful in overcoming social isolation of the homebound.

Rao (1977) lists a great number of advantages for teleteaching systems. A few of these are noted here:

- Teleteaching provides convenient access to the outstanding resource people in various fields.
- It accomodates live or taped lectures; hence it simplifies scheduling.
- Teleteaching acts as a high motivational tool
- It can be used as a break-in medium for student teachers as there is less chance of getting nervous in teaching a remote class.
- The needs of hospitalized and homebound students can be met.

- It permits flexibility in planning and scheduling. One instructor, in a phone booth on the New York Taconic State Parkway, taught a class gathered in Boston.
- It is perhaps the only way to provide quality instruction to students in remote rural areas.
- Classes for a limited number of students can be conducted at different locations simultaneously. In other modes of instruction these small classes might not be economical.

Most of the uses of teleteaching have been isolated examples and not continuing instances. As a technology it may be too complicated to attract frequent users. Its current manifestation is described in chapter 5 under information exchange applications of electronic text. Current configurations rely just as heavily on the phone for oral communication, but they highlight the role of the computer—the more novel of the technologies.

STRENGTHS OF THE
AUDIO MEDIUM FOR INSTRUCTION

What are the unique strengths of audio? Why is it chosen as a stand-alone medium for education? It is clearly a medium that is well suited for music and for language instruction. Both of these are events of the ear. It is not that visual cues cannot add useful information, but they are not essential. Audio is also a good medium for lectures—the transmission of information and even complex concepts that are essentially oral in nature. The more an instructor must depend on visual aids to develop understanding of a point, the more limited is audio. But the advantage of audio over print is that the person speaking can use the emotive powers of the human voice to persuade. In human communication this is an important aspect of instruction. As much as we would like to think that teachers are impartial conveyors of truth, in fact most knowledge is rooted in argument and persuasion, with evidence marshalled to establish a point of view. Audio can capture both the logic of argument and important additional verbal cues as well.

An example illustrates this point. The occasion was a workshop on how to make an outdoor ice rink. It was led by a supervisor from the town's Parks and Recreation Department who, for the last 20 years, had supervised the city's construction of natural ice rinks in local parks. The students had come to learn from this veteran how they could make an ice rink in their own backyard. As they arrived, the instructor passed out a handout with step-by-step instructions. It was an excellent piece of text for the purpose; it covered every detail and every contingency. In the lecture the expert simply reiterated a few of the main points covered in the text.

> Over the years I have found that building up layers of ice by spraying on very thin coats of ice works best. Flooding the yard does not work well. You'll find details about the spraying technique on page three.
>
> Just as I showed in the handout, use a nozzle that looks like this. It will distribute the water evenly.

The reiteration of points came from a person that could be seen and a voice that could be heard. Both belied knowledge backed by experience. Important information was communicated by nuances of tone. Every question raised by the students was answered in the handout, but the instructor patiently answered each question orally, providing reassurance to a group of hesitant novices that all would work out well if they followed the instructions. Technically, the face-to-face class was not needed except that with each question the expert could provide the reassurance that the paper did not convey.

At the extreme, the power of the human voice is seen in the Iranian experience. The Ayatollah Khomenei won the support of the Iranian people from his place of exile in Paris using a collection of audiotapes and a radio station. The message and the voice of the speaker convinced the masses of the righteousness of his cause. Audio is an important aspect of human communication.

In addition to live lectures, audio can transmit many primary source materials, especially those that are oral in nature. This includes interviews with important individuals, human interaction (groups in a meeting), and commentary on events. Audio can even go a long way in conjuring up the visual if listeners have sufficient prior experience. "The Challenge of China and Japan" is an instructional radio series developed under Annenberg/CPB funding. In one segment on life in China a tape recorder is taken to the apartment of a young couple. The husband is a favored intellectual and has acquired comparatively nice housing as a reward. The interviewer relates a verbal description of the dwellings, comparing it with apartments of people of similar stature in America and contrasting it with other homes in China. The listener is able to visualize the home based on extrapolations from experience. It is clearly spacious and elegant by Chinese standards, but cramped and plain by American standards. In an interview with the couple the extent to which such housing is exceptional for someone in China becomes clear. The husband states he has been quite fortunate, and hopes to be able to hold on to this perquisite for a long time.

Finally, the use of aural sound effects can convey much about the character of events. Radio drama has depended on sound effects for a long time. Edward R. Murrow brought the events of World War II to the living rooms of citizens during the war years and, years later, to the study rooms of students too young to know the war years first hand. The sound of howitzers and bombs and breathless soldiers adds a critical dimension to the development of an understanding of the meaning of war.

COMPARING AUDIO AND VIDEO AS MEDIA

If we consider audio as a diminished form of face-to-face communication, it is appropriate to ask how much is lost when the visual channel is taken away. Reid (1977) summarized the available laboratory research in which identical tasks were done in three different ways: face-to-face, oral only (with the communicators within earshot, but out of view), and by telephone. Reid (1977) concluded:

> In information transmission and problem-solving conversations, the withdrawal of vision has no measurable effect of any kind on the outcome of the conversation. In conflict and person perception conversations, however, the medium does affect the outcome . . . [But the] differences do not show the telephone inferior to face-to-face contact in any simple sense. For example, if the objective of negotiation is to change the opinion of the other person, then the telephone could be preferred as producing more opinion change. And while the face-to-face condition produced more favorable and confident evaluations, there is no evidence that these evaluations were any more accurate. (p. 411)

Audio alone is quite powerful to the extent that the tasks examined in this line of research are similar to those in instruction.

A different line of research has compared radio with television.

There are relatively few studies and these are quite recent. Two of note are by Meringoff (1980) and by Beagles-Roos and Gat (1983). Both studies explored story comprehension when the story was presented in an oral form (live reading or radio) and in a televised form. The object was to see what children could recall and infer after their listening/viewing experience. The hypotheses were based on the obvious differences between video and audio. Both media transmit language, sounds, and music. But television also transmits dynamic visual images—an iconic component. Both investigators found subtle but important differences in comprehension between those who viewed the story and those who only heard it. Meringoff (1980) noted:

> Children exposed to the televised story remembered more story actions, offered estimates of shorter elapsed time and distance travelled for carrying out a repeated story event, and relied more on visual content as the basis for inferences. In comparison, children who were read the story in picture book form recalled more story vocabulary, based their inferences more on textual content, general knowledge, and personal experience. (p. 240)

Those who can only listen, it appears, are forced to draw on the subtlety of language in oral presentation, and in so doing are also likely to compare this new knowledge with their own. Beagles-Roos and Gat (1983) add to this:

> Recall of the explicit story content was equivalent across media. However, recall of details from the story was improved with a television presentation. Recognition of expressive language was facilitated by a radio story, whereas [sequencing of pictures of events in the story] was augmented by a television story. The radio story also elevated the use of knowledge unrelated to the story for inferences by younger children and verbal sources for both ages, whereas the television story enhanced inferences based on actions. These findings emphasize the need to consider differential impact of media for conveying explicit and implicit content. (p. 128)

This research establishes the strength of the audio medium for a number of instructional functions, but it highlights as well the point made by Olson and Bruner (1974), "Each form of experience, including the various symbol systems tied to the media, produces a unique pattern of skills for dealing with or thinking about the world" (p. 149).

A reasonable conclusion is that several media may be needed to exploit the instructional goals of a curriculum.

THE AUDIO MEDIUM AND AUDIO TECHNOLOGIES

The Open University is truly multi-media, depending on radio, television, printed text, correspondence, and residential tutorials to teach tens of thousands of students throughout the United Kingdom. Their observations on the uses of a medium and technology is informative. In 1975—4 years after its beginning—a document was issued that listed the "particular appropriate uses of the media" (Open University of Great Britain, 1975). For radio they identified many uses. These can be reduced to five categories:

1. *Primary resource material that is oral in nature:* political speeches, children talking, interviews with eminent people, commentary and interviews at historical events, poets reading their work, musical performances. The notion of primary resource material implies that it is material or evidence to be analyzed as part of some course.

2. *Condensed argument in lecture form:* lectures where an instructor provides an interpretation of primary materials.

3. *Attitude change:* presenting material in a dramatized form so that students can identify with the emotions and viewpoints of the participants.

4. *Flexibility for the instructors:* corrections to aspects of a course contained in another medium (television, print) which is too costly and time-consuming to alter. Remedial tutoring is also possible because audio can be programmed so fast and inexpensively.

5. *Structure:* radio shares with all broadcast media the advantage of a schedule, and this helps distant learners structure their time in a way that audiotape, records, and print media cannot do.

The first three guidelines are based on characteristics of the audio medium. They speak to the nature of aural material. Point four is a mix of medium and technology. Oral presentation—a characteristic of the medium—can be used to correct a narrow aspect of a course, even when video or print was originally judged to be the more appropriate medium for the overall instructional task. On the other hand, flexibility is a technological factor—ease of developing and distributing programs that utilize only the oral medium. The fifth point pertains only to the manner in which radio broadcasts are scheduled on a regular repetitive basis—this is a technological feature. If a radio program is made available on audio cassette, a sixth point can be added—flexibility for learners who can use the material at their own convenience.

Considerations of medium and technology provide different rationales for the choice of audio. Medium issues relate to what is to be learned; here the issue is whether audio is capable of delivering the instructional message to particular audiences. There is strong evidence that audio as a medium is capable of substituting for many instructional tasks such as lecturing and language instruction, and that audio can bring to instruction—either live instruction or distant instruction—a variety of aural material that can enhance understanding. Given the conventions for aural presentations, lectures typically contain material that is less complex than text. When this convention is followed in an audio course, learners who have difficulty mastering text materials have found an advantage to using the audio materials.

Audio is different than video which contains both aural and visual material. It has been shown that learners process video differently than audio materials that contain only an aural component, but the differences are not such that they have clear implications for the design of mediated instruction.

Technology issues relate to the delivery of instruction. Using radio or audiotape to deliver audio materials is a matter of meeting the needs of learners to secure instruction at locations other than an institution that provides it live. It can also be important for giving learners control over the pace of instruction. Audiotape allows a learner the option to hear the material repeatedly until it is understood.

The selection of audio as a medium for instructional programming, and radio or audiotape as a technology for distribution, is defensible on a number of grounds. The selection needs to be made, however, on the basis of the needs of the learning audience.

Chapter 3 _____

Video: Broadcast Television and Videocassettes

The discussion of media in chapter 1 pointed to the important contribution of visuals to any number of learning tasks. In this chapter, we consider the visual medium as carried electronically. The term for this is *video*. For all intents and purposes this means educational programs created on film or videotape and viewed by a learner on a television. The viewer's signal can be derived from either an open-circuit broadcast or a recording.

The early history of educational television showed a predominance of programming that re-created the live classroom. Often referred to as "talking head" programs, they emphasized packaging a master teacher for consumption in other classrooms or, occasionally, by viewers at home. Beginning with "Sesame Street" in 1969, a new breed of television was created that exploited the medium in a new way. Building on the fact that families already looked to television for entertainment, Children's Television Workshop created a series that combined entertainment and instruction, and by doing so captured a home audience that could switch the channel if it thought it was going to watch an "instructional" show. Based on the success of "Sesame Street," and with funding from the federal government, many shows of this type were produced for home and school viewing in the 1970s. Some of the better-known include "The Electric

Company," "Freestyle," and "3-2-1 Contact." At the same time, the Agency for Instructional Television began building a large library of instructional television series for use predominantly in the classroom. The programs were paid for by consortia of state and (in Canada) provincial educational agencies. Well-known among these are "Self-Incorporated," "Trade-Offs," and "ThinkAbout."

In 1969, the British government funded the Open University—an effort to make a college education available to all citizens of England using television as one of the central vehicles in a multi-media operation. It currently has more than 3,000 video programs and an equal number of audio shows in its library. The programs are keyed to courses ranging from math and chemistry to English and anthropology. More recently in the United States a large donation by Walter Annenberg made possible the production of a number of television series that provided instruction in a variety of post-secondary subject areas, including English ("The Write Course"), government ("Congress, We the People"; "Constitution: That Delicate Balance"), biology ("The Brain"), and computers ("The New Literacy").

This chapter reviews the evidence for instructional effectiveness of programming in the video medium. It pays special attention to the conditions under which television has been shown to be an effective instructional tool.

TELEVISION FOR CHILDREN

Television is a pervasive technology in both homes and schools. Given this ecological fact, it is appropriate to investigate two possibilities. Can television contribute something to instruction when it is integrated into a larger educational effort such as classroom instruction? Also, can broadcasting educational television to homes make a unique contribution when it is not integrated into the school curriculum? These questions can be addressed by looking at the research on several children's shows. Some of the research is well known, such as that on "Sesame Street." But research on shows such as "The Electric Company," "Freestyle," and "ThinkAbout" has not had wide circulation among educators. These are all important series because each is an example of an experiment to explore the limits of the video medium to teach cognitive and affective goals. Modeled on the precedent-setting "Sesame Street," each series carefully combines entertainment and instruction in an artfully engineered package that aims to entertain—in order to attract and hold viewer attention—while it teaches. Although these shows are often used in classrooms, "Electric Company," "Freestyle," and "3-2-1 Contact" are designed specifically for home audiences as well. Getting the attention of children in this environment is very difficult given the competition of cartoons or not watching television at all. Home viewers would be intolerant of overly didactic or talking head presentations. "ThinkAbout" is designed for use only in classrooms, but the entertain-and-teach characteristic is clearly there.

What have previous research reviews concluded about television's potential? Under the right conditions television can teach a variety of cognitive and affective concepts to some viewers. The conditions include attentive viewing, adult mediation (encouragement to view and explanation of the content), post-viewing rehearsal of desired responses, and social support. These will be recognized as factors that enhance any type of classroom learning. In short, earlier research showed that television has the potential to augment instruction, but it does not do it as effectively by itself as it does when teachers provide an interface between the program and learners.

Teaching Cognitive Skills

"Sesame Street".   Because it set the course for subsequent entertain-and-teach series, a brief review of "Sesame Street" is useful. The series made its debut in November 1969. The original set of programs was designed to teach preschoolers literacy or preliteracy skills such as letter and number recognition and certain relational terms. Using a test that measured just these skills, it was found that viewing the first season of shows led to gains in each of these dimensions (Ball & Bogatz, 1970). The gains were similar for boys and girls, Spanish- and English-speaking children, and rural and urban children. Younger children learned more than older, and advantaged children more than disadvantaged children. Also, children who were encouraged to view learned more than those who were not encouraged.

A second round of research found that, after 2 years, frequent viewers not only learned the "Sesame Street" content, but also had higher scores on a test of general verbal IQ (Ball & Bogatz, 1973). In addition, when they began attending school frequent viewers had more positive attitudes about school.

Some reservations have been expressed about these conclusions

(Cook et al., 1975). The controversy centers on the potential of "Sesame Street" to be a stand-alone teacher. Critics have noted that parental encouragement and supplementary materials were essential to achieving the effects observed. In truth, the educational effects were much larger for viewers who were encouraged by an adult, but modest effects were found for "mere" viewing as well. These findings show the potential of this form of television to teach, but they also show that personal characteristics of the viewer and the viewer's context influence the amount learned.

In subsequent production of new segments for "Sesame Street" additional learning goals were added, including affective ones. Their impact is not reviewed here, but a discussion can be found in Johnston and Ettema (1986).

"The Electric Company".   The next project of Children's Television Workshop (CTW) was "The Electric Company". Introduced in 1971, the series was aimed at children in the early elementary grades who were deficient in certain reading skills. It focused on three basic reading strategies: blending, "chunking" of letter groups, and scanning for patterns. Viewers were supposed to learn how to discriminate vowels from consonants, scan text for typical word structures, read for meaning and use the context of a sentence to determine the meaning of an ambiguous word. The intriguing aspect of "The Electric Company" is the choice of the video medium to teach skills in decoding the print medium.

The evaluation of "The Electric Company" provided some interesting insights on the strengths and limits of television (see, for example, Ball & Bogatz, 1973; Bryant, Alexander, & Brown, 1983). Consider the children who viewed the shows as a captive audience in schools. Here, teachers insured that they watched, discussed the shows, and practiced the concepts. These children demonstrated real growth. First graders showed improved performance on all scales of a test that measured blending, chunking, scanning for patterns, and reading for meaning—all skills taught directly by the show. Second graders showed less improvement, and third and fourth graders improved only their blending and a few chunking skills. Gains were greatest for those most in need of help—those in the bottom half of their classes in reading ability—and were unrelated to gender or race. In short, learning definitely did occur when viewing was insured, and when teachers supplied additional learning materials and helped the children to rehearse the material presented on television. Impressive is the fact that gains were noted by comparing "The Electric Company" viewers with students who were also studying reading in school, but were different only in not watching "The Electric Company."

An attempt was made to measure the impact of home viewing; but this group viewed about the same amount as a control group, so the effectiveness of home viewing could not be measured. However, it was clear that the challenge would be to attract and hold an audience for a number of shows sufficient to have a measurable impact on their reading skills.

The research on "Sesame Street" and "The Electric Company" indicates that television can indeed teach certain academic skills to children ranging in age from 3 to 10. But its teaching ability is limited in the absence of support materials and an interested adult who can encourage viewing and extend the lesson. Obviously, it cannot teach at all if children do not view the shows. This underscores the distinction between television's capacity to teach, and television as stand-alone teacher. As good as the CTW strategy of entertain-and-teach may be, attracting and maintaining a home audience in the face of competing activities in a child's life is a difficult task at best. Nielsen data for 1980 showed an incredibly high percentage of TV homes with the set tuned at some time or other to "The Electric Company"— 91%. This is not the same, however, as showing that there is a large group of children who view the shows day after day in a fashion consistent enough to result in measurable change in their cognitive abilities. This is not to be critical of "The Electric Company"; it can clearly deliver an important educational message to viewers. Rather, it highlights the difficulty of depending on the home as the educational context.

"ThinkAbout".   Created by the Agency for Instructional Television (AIT, 1982), the "ThinkAbout" television series is sixty 15-minute episodes:

> designed to strengthen the reasoning skills of fifth and sixth graders and to reinforce their language arts, mathematics, and study skills. The series unifies the basics by focusing on their common denominator: thinking. Each program is a tool for applying one group of basic skills to a reasoning or problem-solving task children face in and out of school.

There are 13 program clusters on topics such as finding alternatives, estimating and approximating, giving and getting meaning, collecting information, and so on. As an example, in the show "Brainstorming" the student council is asked to come up with ways to deal with a phantom painter who has been defacing the walls of the school. Council members generate some useful alternatives by following a four-step brainstorming process promoted by the series' curriculum. Such a show is designed to be used in a classroom where the teacher can follow up with practice and application of the brainstorming steps.

The series is quite ambitious, not just in its scope but in its attempt to harness the medium of television to teach some very abstract and difficult skills. But it was created for this very purpose. Upper elementary teachers around the country indicated that teaching basic thinking skills was their most difficult academic challenge. AIT responded with this television series and accompanying guide.

Did students who spent 2 hours a week with "ThinkAbout" improve their basic thinking skills? To a very limited extent, according to the research. Sanders (1983) states:

> Tests used in the study yielded limited evidence on goal attainment by students in "ThinkAbout" classrooms. The tests [California Test of Basic Skills] detected no unusual patterns of basic skill acceleration. The "ThinkAbout" instruments provided spotty documentation of the development of thinking, self-management, and communication skills. Nevertheless, it is worth noting that the introduction of two hours per week of problem-solving and study skills instruction did not diminish basic skills learning and added a new element to the classroom. (p. 6)

The research on "ThinkAbout" is limited in two ways. First, responding to pressures from the very people who wanted the series created, the criterion of its effectiveness was established as improved performance on a general test of basic skills. This criterion was unrealistic. Second, effects were measured after only the first year of uncontrolled use—an insufficient amount of time for teachers to adapt their curriculum to the new content and teach the material as its designers intended (see Johnston, 1981, for a discussion of appropriate strategies to assess new curriculum products).

One of the most valuable contributions of the research on "ThinkAbout" is a series of case studies on how "ThinkAbout" was used in classrooms (see Cohn, 1982; Hart-Landsberg, 1982; Wolcott, 1982). They are invaluable reading for anyone with an understanding of classroom life and the range of ways in which technology's impact is shaped by it. They illustrate how some classroom teachers understand how to teach problem solving, but simply lack the curriculum materials to guide them. "ThinkAbout" filled this need and these teachers were able to conduct stimulating class discussion after each show. In many other classrooms, basic notions of problem solving were not understood by the teachers, and they never extended the televised "trigger" lesson into subsequent class activities.

Strictly speaking, it appears that "ThinkAbout" is not effective as a teacher of basic thinking skills. Another interpretation is that "ThinkAbout" took the most difficult of intellectual concepts and was able to teach no better than the teachers who had asked for help in this academic domain. But, its effectiveness might be measured in other ways. Sanders notes that 84% of the 489 teachers using the series said that "ThinkAbout" presented complex ideas better in 15 minutes than the teacher could, and 88% reported that the shows stimulated discussion in class. The series also had a sizeable impact on the curriculum; teachers and students spent up to 2 hours a week on problem solving throughout the school year—something they had not done previously.

Teaching Affective Goals

"Freestyle".   There is more to education than expanding academic skills. Much of the process of education is focused on expanding a child's social skills and developing social attitudes appropriate to a democratic society. Can television help in this domain? Research in the early 1970s made it clear that it was possible, given the proper imbedding of "prosocial" messages in the television shows, and the usual requirements of attentive viewing. During the mid- and late 1970s there were many conscious attempts to harness television's prosocial potential. A notable example of this is "Freestyle," a 13-part dramatic series for 9- to 12-year-olds. It was designed to alter sex-role stereotypes regarding appropriate behavior for boys and girls. This goal was judged to be important if girls were to find social support for making the educational and career choices appropriate in a society where half the adult females hold jobs outside the home. The research on the effects of this show add more to our understanding of when and how the medium can be used to best advantage. (See Johnston & Ettema, 1982, for an extended treatment of the "Freestyle" research.)

The shows were tested in three different settings to disentangle some of the ambiguous findings of earlier research regarding home viewing. In one setting, students watched all the shows in school, but there was no discussion or additional activities. This was a test of mere viewing. It does not represent a typical way that a television series is used, but its use in this fashion shows what viewing the complete set of shows might accomplish. In a second setting, students watched the shows at home. Once a week on the day the show was broadcast, the teacher reminded students to watch, but the shows were never discussed in school. This situation approximates natural home viewing with a level of encouragement that schools could realistically use if a broadcast television series were identified as valuable. In a third setting, students watched all the shows in school; in addition, the teacher led a discussion of each show and guided the students through related activities. This situation is typical of school use of television.

The 7,000 students in the research were asked questions in three domains, corresponding to topics addressed in the shows.

- *Beliefs* about boys' and girls' competence in nontraditional activities—girls in sports and boys in child care, for example;
- *Attitudes* about boys and girls engaging in nontraditional activities ("Is it a good idea for girls to play football?");
- *Interest* in doing various activities, some of which would be nontraditional for their gender.

In total, from 168 questions 20 indices of impact were derived—8 belief and 8 attitude measures, and 4 interest measures.

Consider first those children who merely viewed the shows in schools. Among female viewers there were significant changes on half of the belief and attitude measures, and increased personal liking for mechanical activities—a nontraditional activity for females. The changes in male viewers were fewer; they changed on only a quarter of the belief and attitude measures, and expressed no increased interest in the activity domain considered most nontraditional for boys—nurturant activities such as child care and helping around home. There were no cases of a negative effect (e.g., males or females expressing more sexist beliefs and attitudes).

Among those who were asked to view the shows at home, effects were very small and were found for only the heaviest viewers: 7 or more shows for females and 10 or more for males. Heavy viewing resulted in changes regarding only one topic: girls doing mechanical activities (e.g., girls repairing a bike or building a model; adult women being auto mechanics). Among heavy viewers (7 or more of the 13 shows), females and males alike became more accepting of girls doing this activity; females also showed increased personal interest in mechanics.

These and other results showed a number of things about simply viewing television without having a teacher provide additional guidance. Merely viewing a modest amount of purposefully constructed prosocial dramatic programming *can* alter beliefs, attitudes and even interests of viewers. Although the effects of home viewing were small, none of them were negative; for example, boys were not alienated by the notion of girls aspiring to achieve in traditionally male domains. Other findings include these. Belief and attitude change can generalize beyond show-specific concepts. Size of effects vary with viewer predisposition—girls changed more than boys in this case. Effects are more easily achieved with some topics than others (e.g., the highly concrete subject of mechanics is easier to influence than the subtleties of assertiveness or leadership). Finally, effects are more easily achieved with some types of outcomes than others—attitudes and beliefs are changed more easily than personal preferences.

Results for those who viewed and discussed the shows in school provide additional insights about television's potential. These viewers showed very large changes on most of the measures. Typically, the size of the changes were double that of heavy viewing alone, although in two instances mere viewing was equal to viewing-plus-discussion. These large effects were also found to persist to a great extent 9 months later.

Why is the classroom context so much more effective? Class discussion probably does two things. First, in the realm of belief and attitude change, confronting the issues—in this case, girls hearing and confronting boys, and vice versa—is more powerful than simply watching a confrontation on the screen. Second, adult-mediated discussion can make up for deficiencies in dramatic production. The "Freestyle" research shows that, given a set of affective goals, television can achieve a lot, but there are tradeoffs. To achieve with home viewing the large effect sizes found with school viewing requires much more programming and many more efforts to encourage home viewing. On the other hand, as the "ThinkAbout" research shows, mobilizing schools to use the programming effectively is also difficult and very costly.

TELEVISION FOR ADULTS

Until very recently, little attention has been given in the United States to creating educational television for adults. There are several series that are educational in the broadest sense—series such as "Nova" and the collection of National Geographic specials; but these are not designed to carry sufficient instructional material to qualify as a major part of formal coursework for either distant learners or learners matriculating in post high school institutions. There is a large collection of video produced for specific courses at various institutions. Some of the older products were reviewed by Chu and Schramm (1979). More recent reviews have included research on shows created since 1966. Over the years, these reviews have sought to compare the overall effects of visual-based instruction (VBI) with conventional live teaching. Although such reviews are useful, they are limited in what they can tell us about how to create and deliver instructionally effective educational television. Despite this limitation, it is worthwhile to report on what the most recent reviews have found.

Overall Assessments

To generalize across a number of studies of VBI, the more recent reviews have utilized the now-popular method of meta-analysis in which the results of each study are converted to a common metric, effect size (ES). *Effect size* is a measure of the difference between a control group that did not have VBI and an experimental group that did. ES is expressed in terms of standard deviation units. An ES of .17 is quite small and unimportant, whereas an ES of .33 is modest but important. To interpret the figure more easily it can be converted to percentiles. An effect size of .33—one third of a standard deviation difference between a control group and a group receiving VBI—translates to the video group being at the 63rd percentile compared to the control group at the 50th percentile.

The most recent meta-analysis of VBI was reported by Cohen, Ebeling, and Kulik (1981). (Kulik and his colleagues have conducted meta-analytic reviews of several media and they are discussed in the next chapter.) In this review, 74 studies of VBI were analyzed. It was found that, on average, VBI had only slightly larger effects on student achievement than conventional teaching. The ES average = .15. This number is not statistically significant; but it shows that VBI can result in as good achievement as live instruction, and the tendency in the data is toward exceeding the results from live teaching. Cohen et al. (1981) state:

> In the typical study, visual-based instruction had no special effect on course completion, student attitudes, or the correlation between aptitude and achievement. Students were equally likely to complete visual-based and conventional classes; their attitudes toward the two kinds of classes were very similar; and aptitude played a strong role in determining student achievement in each kind of class. (p. 26)

Overall, this review found that 74% of the studies of student achievement reported no significant difference. This is the same as Chu and Schramm reported in 1967. (Chu & Schramm, 1979, is the fourth printing of a book they wrote 12 years earlier.) Of the studies that did find a significant difference, Chu and Schramm found only 44% favoring VBI, whereas Cohen and his colleagues found 76%. Cohen et al. (1981) conclude that gains from VBI "are substantially smaller than those reported in the typical study of Keller's personalized system of instruction [Kulik, Kulik, & Cohen, 1979b] and slightly smaller than those reported for audiotutorial instruction [Kulik, Kulik, & Cohen, 1979a], computer-based instruction [Kulik, Kulik & Cohen, 1980], and print-based programmed instruction [Kulik, Cohen & Ebeling, 1980]" (Cohen et al., 1981, p. 34). This seems quite reasonable. Most VBI is designed to be an enhanced information presentation. If the VBI version of a course can be at least equivalent to a live presentation, then it has enabled the classroom to be extended beyond the institutional walls. The Keller Plan and other approaches that were evaluated all add a tutorial component that could be expected to produce higher achievement by virtue of their attention to individual differences in comprehension.

Cohen and his colleagues reported only one finding that comments on the medium itself. They found "moderate ES" for studies in which visual aid provided feedback for teacher training or other skill acquisition. "It seems that for this type of implementation visual media are more likely to make a unique contribution to student learning" (Cohen et al., 1981, p. 34).

This type of meta-analytic research provides evidence that VBI can be at least as good as live instruction, although it tells us little about the types of programming or delivery conditions that contribute to this outcome. In general terms, then, it seems that the choice of video for instruction should be based on a demonstrated need for instruction to be delivered electronically instead of live. "Sesame Street" reaches into homes and provides school readiness skills that are not being delivered in other ways. Can educational television for adults be similarly justified? If one looks at the typical student that enrolls for a telecourse the answer is yes. In a study done for the Corporation for Public Broadcasting, Brey and Grigsby (1984) report that the typical student enrolling in a telecourse differs from those taking traditional courses in that they are older, more likely to be women, have dependents at home, be employed, and report that they are taking the course because it can be more easily accomodated to their schedule. There is a need, then, among this group to have a form of distant learning that is equivalent to what is available in the traditional live course.

Lessons from Britain's Open University

In the late 1960s it was judged that the existing institutions of higher education in England were unable to provide as much opportunity for post-secondary education as the public demanded. The government responded by creating a university for distant learning in which television would play a role. Students use a combination of special correspondence texts, television, radio or audio-cassettes, and—in some instances—home experiment kits. For some courses there are compulsory 1-week summer schools, and in many locations a student can hire a tutor. Each student is assigned a correspondence tutor, who marks assignments and advises the student. There are monitored examinations at the end of the course. For most courses, the heart of the instruction is a correspondence text, occasionally supplemented by other print material. At most, students get one 25-minute television program per week (or 32 in a full course). Some courses may have only one television show per month, and a few courses have no television programs at all.

Throughout its brief history, Open University staff have conducted research studies in connection with the courses. A number of the studies, summarized by Bates (1983), are informative with respect to several of the issues raised in this book. The Open University uses multiple media for each course with the notion that a topic is dealt with differently depending on the medium for which it is developed. As a result, students using all of the media that comprise a course will process and use the knowledge in multiple ways, and this is useful.

Several studies indicate how the possibilities available for a medium will be utilized only to the extent that several contextual factors are consonant with the goals of the program's designers. One way that television is used by the Open University is to present case studies. In many courses the correspondence texts are very theoretical, analytical, and didactic. A television case study can present concrete, real-world situations and provide opportunities to apply, generalize, and evaluate the concepts presented in the correspondence texts. Pedagogically, the goal is quite defensible. But, in one study it was estimated that only about one third of the students understood this to be the purpose of the case studies and knew how to use them in this way. The mind set of most of the students relative to instructional television is that its function is to explain concepts that are inadequately dealt with in the text. Rather than trying to apply what was learned in the text, these students viewed the shows looking for new concepts to be memorized. By design, none were to be found in the case studies.

Students are very pragmatic learners. Their use of the television and radio programs depended greatly on whether they believed they would be tested on the material. If early tests or study-guide questions suggested the shows were not integral to achievement, students would watch the programs less often. The problem is twofold. It is understandable that students would make such pragmatic judgments, but can't the tests be revised to include such questions? The Open University found it difficult to get instructors to do this; many of them found it too difficult or unimportant, even though they had initially encouraged the production of case studies for this purpose.

Two other factors were important in explaining whether students bothered to watch the television programs. If the material was integrated well with the printed text, they would be more likely to watch. But integration is a complex problem. Students tend to be about 3 weeks behind in their readings. If the television show requires application of concepts from the readings, students who are behind will not see the relevance. On the production side, they find it quite difficult to coordinate production of print and video materials. The print material has much longer lead times, and the video production may not be available in time to write text material tailored to the video production.

Clearly, to learn from the video productions requires that students can easily view the shows. Over the years, the Open University has carefully chosen time slots for broadcasts to fit the diverse needs of their student body. As the number of courses has grown and the demands for air time increased, the ideal broadcast schedule has not been maintained. Data collected from students on their viewing habits show that there was a sharp drop off in viewing when these adjustments were made to the schedule. Delivery, then, of even the best program is a critical factor affecting learning outcomes.

An important discovery of the Open University relates to what type of students find the radio and television programs useful. In general, students with higher grades use the programs more than those with lower grades. This may well relate to the different motivation of those who get higher grades. However, the weaker students (based on overall grade-point average) who do watch or listen to the programs rate the broadcasts as more helpful than do the more successful students. Having investigated other possibilities, the staff concludes that some students have difficulty with text; they have not been successful readers in their past academic experiences. These students look to audio and video for a simplification of the material.

In general, the Open University is committed to using multiple media as part of their distant learning program. But their experience highlights the difficulty of orchestrating the many elements of medium, technology, programming, the learner's context, and the learner's mind set in such a way that learning will result.

CREATING EFFECTIVE PROGRAMMING FOR VIDEO

When video is used to simply record a lecture, the videographer can do little to affect the message conveyed by the speaker. But video is typically used in more complex ways as illustrated in the series reviewed earlier in this chapter. If one ignores for a moment the contextual factors that influence a viewer's attention and comprehension, what is known about creating video that can achieve particular educational goals under the proper conditions? The answer is complex. There are a large number of studies that examine the role of factors such as formal elements (visual tricks, audio enhancements), program formats, modeling strategies, structural elements (e.g., the temporal separation of plot events; the use of action to highlight a message), and form-content relationships (e.g., the use of drama instead of lecture to convey certain messages). In the last 20 years many lessons have been learned about small elements important in creating programming that has the potential to be educationally effective (see, for example, Johnston & Ettema, 1986; Kozma, 1986; Mielke & Chen, 1983). But the research results are limited in what they tell future producers about creating effective video. A video production is too complicated to be engineered by formulae drawn from collections of individual studies. Johnston and Ettema (1986) state:

> The notion that television is a bundle of discrete elements which can be disentangled and then rewoven as desired is, at best, simplistic. The meaning of television rests on a set of symbolic conventions. But these conventions are rooted not only in the history of television, but also in the history of cinema and storytelling itself. The symbolic conventions can be manipulated toward a variety of ends, but this manipulation will probably always be more an act of creation than a feat of engineering. (p. 155)

Although precise principles cannot be stated, much has been learned about the importance of a particular production process. Educational television requires the orchestration of different types of expertise—video production, instructional design, and content—coupled with a formative evaluation strategy that constantly checks the educated guesses of the experts against the responses of the intended audience. Typically, for a new series, evaluators will select samples of the target audience to measure appeal and comprehension of the production at various stages ranging from actor selection and storyboards to completed segments of shows. When such information is made available to the producers in a timely fashion, corrections can be made to insure the production of the most effective series possible.

Chapter 4 _____

Electronic Text and Graphics: Computers

Electronic text and graphics is the electronic version of printed text. To understand electronic text, a few points must be made about print. For centuries, printed text has been the primary source material for formal instruction. The term *print* usually includes graphics and pictures as well as words; together these make a very versatile medium for learning and instruction. It is ideally suited for the presentation of facts to be learned and remembered. The mind can process only limited quantities of information at a time. A printed book keeps new material available indefinitely, so each learner can process chunks of material at a pace suitable to her or his skill, motivation, and time available. Print is also a good medium for the presentation of complex algorithms such as the calculation of statistical variance or the elaboration of concepts such as democracy or technology. As with large quantities of verbal information, the human mind needs the opportunity presented by the fixed medium of print to read and reread difficult material in order to process and assimilate it to the mind's unique schema. For similar material, audio is often inefficient; listeners have limited ability to hold the complex information in short-term memory. Video is often inappropriate too because many concepts do not have an inherently visual aspect to them, and the weight of the explanation falls back on the audio track. Because the production of video is expensive relative to print, it must be reserved for situations that require what video can do best. Printed text, then, is a medium capable of communicating a wide range of ideas in an efficient compact form. Its weaknesses for education are twofold. One, it is passive; a learner must engage the material and know how to efficiently process the information contained there. Second, the printed word is immutable. In a time of rapidly changing information any single utterance can be outdated in a short period of time. It is in these areas that electronic text and graphics can contribute.

The Limits of Printed Text for Instruction

Educators have noted for a long time the inadequacy of printed text alone to carry the burden of instruction. It has two weaknesses; text is usually written as a single integrated set of ideas at a particular level of complexity. For a group of learners with varying background and abilities, ideas need to be presented in a variety of ways, reflecting the diversity of backgrounds that readers bring to a text. As an author increases the variety and depth of presentation, a single text becomes unwieldy in size. The solution in print is to make available a variety of texts on the same topic, each geared to audiences with a different average level of academic skill and prior knowledge. But it is still geared to an audience with some average characteristic (ability or completion of some prerequisite course). Within any group there is often greater variability than any text can meet.

A second weakness of print is that learners can read without assimilating the ideas. Some lack the cognitive strategies to identify salient points, comprehend what is written or remember what is read. Interspersing salient questions throughout a text can help to cue learners to important points, but the learner's response to such questions must be evaluated by an expert to ascertain what additional guidance is needed. Frequent assessment by an instructor can provide the necessary feedback to tell learners if they have successfully grasped an idea; but then the instructional task has demanded resources beyond the text itself.

The programmed textbook is one answer to these problems. It contains three elements. First, there is instructional text that carries the main burden of information transfer. Second, there are multiple-choice questions interspersed through the text that assess a learner's comprehension of each major point. They are arranged so that a learner cannot proceed to additional text without answering the question; and each answer directs the learner to a different page of text. The answer choices include a correct response and one or more answers chosen because they represent particular types of misunderstandings frequently exhibited by learners. Selection of the correct response results in the learner continuing with the main instructional text. Selection of one of the incorrect responses leads to one of several possible remedial frames of text designed to remedy the learner's specific problem in comprehending the ideas. The remedial branches of a programmed text provide the third critical element of a programmed text.

But a programmed text on all but the simplest of instructional topics is unwieldy in size. For this and other reasons, this format of printed text never captured the imagination of teachers or the textbook industry. One reason is that any type of self-paced instruction requires tedious analysis of the learning task by an author and the development of complex branches for remediation. Such development finds little reward in academia, especially when most teachers (the ones who choose textbooks) see the diagnostic and remediation task as their primary responsibility in the classroom.

The Character of Electronic Text

The invention of the computer has made possible totally fluid text and graphics. Given the proper instructions, a computer can reassemble letters and words in an infinite number of ways. With appropriate memory devices (magnetic or laser), the computer is capable of storing very compactly virtually all the world's collection of text and graphics, and recalling it instantly in whatever sequence is judged most desirable. Electronic text can be distributed on disks of various types to be physically manipulated on a user's own computer, or the information can be stored in one location and accessed by geographically disparate users over high-speed telephone lines.

As a medium, electronic text shares many of the characteristics of printed text. Words can be used to convey a wide variety of knowledge from the presentation of simple declarative knowledge to the explanation of complex propositions and procedural rules. Most systems that transport electronic text also have some capacity for graphics, and these can be used to summarize abstract concepts as needed.

Essential to the production of electronic text is an integrated circuit that routes the selection of electronic text to be displayed according to instructions in the software. The instructions determine which text will be seen on a screen. At its simplest, the instructions can produce a linear flow of text similar to a printed book. However, the same circuitry has the potential to collect and evaluate information from the user and utilize this information to change the flow of text presentation. It is this logical and branching capability inherent in the technology of electronic text systems that distinguishes this medium from other electronic media. At its simplest, it can duplicate the programmed text, but hide the wealth of remedial branches that make printed programmed texts unwieldy.

Computer-assisted instruction was first developed in the 1960s on large mainframe computers. With the introduction of the microcomputer in the 1970s a form of electronic programmed instruction began to flourish. This included drill-and-practice and simple tutorial programs. Today there are more than 8,000 instructional software programs listed in *TESS: The Educational Software Selector* published by the Educational Products Information Exchange. The design problem for computer-based teaching is the same as print-based programmed instruction, so why is it flourishing when print-based programmed instruction is not? One explanation is the appeal of the microcomputer as a tool. For the learner, the computer has great intrinsic motivational qualities that make it appealing in a way that programmed text is not. (See Lepper & Malone, in press; and Malone, 1980.) There is a fascination with programming a computer that makes the development of a tutorial program attractive when compared with the tedium of programmed text. In the early days, programs rarely covered very much material, so the scope of work was much less than developing a complete textbook. A lone designer in a basement could put a piece of programmed instruction onto a floppy disk and distribute it to fellow colleagues or members of a computing club. He did not need to find a publisher and get involved in all that is entailed in stocking and promoting texts in the print medium.

THE VARIED EDUCATIONAL USES
OF ELECTRONIC TEXT

Today, electronic text is being used in education in a wide variety of ways. It is used not only for tutoring and drill-and-practice programs, but also for interactive simulations, electronic spreadsheets, storage of bibliographic materials in remote data bases, and communicating between learners in distant locations. These diverse applications can be usefully categorized by the communicational intent of the teacher or learner. The intent speaks to the issue of its role in the teaching–learning process. (This conceptualization is a modification of one proposed by Allen, Hickey, & Molise, 1985.) The focus of this book is on the media used for instructional purposes. With electronic text, however, it is more difficult to draw the distinction than with audio and video.

There are three major categories of intent: instructional, instrumental, and informational (see Table 4.1). *Instructional applications* are those in which the software is being used in ways specifically designed to instruct a learner. Generically, these can be referred to as computer-based instruction (CBI). There are several subcategories of CBI. The most obvious applications in this category are the tutorial ones commonly referred to as computer-assisted instruction (CAI). Included are drill-and-practice in which learners are tested for mastery of material already learned from conventional sources. A variant is the true tutorial in which the software presents new information as well as testing for mastery. Another subcategory of tutorial applications is computer-managed instruction (CMI). Here the computer assesses student mastery, but—instead of presenting instructional material in electronic form—it directs the learner to appropriate materials in other media such as print, audio, or video.

Another instructional application of electronic text is the *interactive simulation.* A rule-driven environment is presented to the learner; the learner's goal is to manipulate the environment in a way that demonstrates an understanding of the many complex rules that govern it. Thus, a medical student in a cardiac arrest simulation program can apply her or his knowledge of how the ailing heart responds to various forms of treatment. If the correct treatment is chosen the simulated patient "lives"; if not the patient "dies."

A special form of simulation is computer programming. A computer program can be thought of as a set of instructions that direct a rule-driven system—the computer's central processing unit—to accomplish a particular task. When programming is taught as a skill akin to typing, the intent may be only to add to the students' repertoire of tool-like skills. However, successfully writing a program involves the process of analyzing the task that the program is to accomplish, planning the flow of the program, testing out a particular solution and debugging the errors. In short, programming can be thought of as a simulation of a general problem-solving environment. It is sometimes taught with the intent more of enhancing mental

TABLE 4.1
Applications of Electronic Text and Graphics
Classified by Communicational Intent

Instructional Applications

Tutoring: Drill-and-practice, computer-assisted instruction (CAI), computer-managed instruction (CMI). Intelligent CAI (ICAI); expert systems and artificial intelligence (AI)

Interactive simulations

Computer programming as training in problem-solving

Instrumental Applications

Tool uses including data base management, word processing, electronic spreadsheets, statistical and other mathematical calculators, and computer-aided design

Computer programming taught with the primary purpose of developing a student's programming skill to use subsequently to program a computer to accomplish some task

Laboratory tool to collect physical data from experiments (e.g., temperature or voltage)

Informational Applications

Retrieving information: Data bases for stored information (bibliographies, library catalogs, stock prices, etc.)

Exchanging information: Messages and bulletin boards. Computer conferencing

---

problem-solving skills than developing a new set of applications skills.

Instrumental applications are those in which the computer is programmed to accomplish a particular task that is not itself instructional. These are sometimes referred to as tool uses of the computer (Taylor, 1980). A database program is designed to store information for easy sorting and retrieval. Electronic spreadsheets allow the formula-driven manipulation of information contained in a ledger or spreadsheet format. Other applications include word-processing and text-analysis programs, and the use of the computer as a data-collection device. Programming itself is a kit of tools that can be used to create yet other tools to solve a variety of problems. These many uses are appropriately classified under instrumental applications if the instructor's intent is to teach students how to operate the tool for subsequent use. Thus, if a student is taught to use a spreadsheet so that he or she can utilize this tool in business settings, then it is an instrumental application of the computer. If a teacher takes the same spreadsheet program and carefully enters formulas into some of the cells to simulate a particular scientific algorithm, then the application becomes an instructional one. Similarly for teaching programming—if it is being taught to give students the skills to write their own tools, then it is an instrumental application. If it is being used as Seymour Papert (1980) and others would hope—as a tool of the intellect to help expand the problem-solving skills of students—then programming is being used as an instructional application.

Informational applications are those in which the computer is being used to link users to sources of stored information or to other people. Accessing a bibliographic database in the DIALOG system is an informational application, as is using the computer to access an on-line library catalog. Participating in a computer conference set up to link students in a course is also an informational application. Although learning may occur in communication between student and teacher, or among students, it is the humans, not the computer, that are doing the teaching. The computer is only facilitating the flow of information.

INSTRUCTIONAL APPLICATIONS: TUTORING AND SIMULATIONS

Computer software for instruction has a history of about 25 years. In the 1960s and 1970s software was developed almost exclusively for mainframe computers, and students accessed the programs by sitting at terminals. The limitations in technology in these 2 decades meant that most computer-based instruction occurred in facilities adjacent to the computers; this was rarely a public school classroom or home. Another characteristic of the early software is that it was predominantly of the drill-and-practice variety.

The introduction of the microcomputer in the 1970s and its rapid proliferation in schools in the 1980s changed the availability of computing power for schools. In the 1980s an individual school or classroom could have access to an Apple II microcomputer with greater computing power than the mainframe computers in use a decade earlier. With the proliferation of hardware came a comparable expansion of the number of instructional programs available for use in schools. The 1985 edition of *TESS: The Educational Software Selector,* published by the Educational Products Information Exchange (EPIE) Institute, lists almost 8,000 programs for microcomputers. But the vast majority of these are still of the drill-and-practice variety. True tutorial software—a more complex instructional and programming task, requiring fairly sophisticated computer systems—is only beginning to appear in the mid 1980s.

Most of the microcomputer software has been created for elementary school children; the supply tapers off very quickly as one moves to junior and senior high school and into college. Using principles of motivation and reinforcement as they relate to persistence at a task, drill-and-practice programs represent what the computer does best and humans do poorly: repetition of questions at a level appropriate to the learner's skills and with a patience unmatched by any but the most caring parent. In the domain of rote skills, the computer would appear to be an ideal tutor for developing automaticity with the memorization of concepts and the application of simple rules and procedures.

Taken together, the common judgment is that the majority of microcomputer software available today is of limited utility for regular classroom use. The tasks, rewards, or pacing do not fit curricular needs, or they do not match most students' style of learning, but a small number of the programs are quite good at what they do. As developers emerged from their basements and joined with others in corporate endeavors reflecting the complexities inherent in developing good teaching in any medium, reasonable products have begun to appear.

The rapid evolution of software presents serious limitations to a scientific assessment of the medium's contribution to instruction. Most of the studies now available were conducted in the 1960s or 1970s using students who were taught with drill-and-practice software developed for mainframe or large minicomputers.

The Computer as Tutor

In the last 15 years there has been a spate of review articles summarizing the results of numerous studies of CBI. An examination of 11 major review studies published between 1972 and 1986 leads to several generalizations about the effectiveness of computer-assisted instruction (Bangert-Drowns, Kulik, & Kulik, 1985; Burns & Bozeman, 1981;

Edwards, Norton, Taylor, Weiss, & Dusseldorp, 1975; Hartley, 1978; Jamison, Suppes, & Wells, 1974; Kulik, Bangert, & Williams, 1983; Kulik & Bangert-Drowns, 1983; Kulik et al., 1980b; Kulik, Kulik, & Bangert-Drowns, 1985; Niemic & Walberg, 1986; Vinsonhaler & Bass, 1972). But before reviewing the results, consider the characteristics of the studies themselves because they serve to qualify the conclusions. The following generalizations are based on an examination of the 175 studies summarized in the elementary, secondary, and college level meta-analyses done by Kulik and his colleagues.

Almost all of the studies were conducted before 1980. This means that the hardware and software used for these studies looks significantly different than what is found today. In elementary-school studies most of the studies evaluated drill-and-practice applications in mathematics. The computer was used for an average of 26 hours: 15 minutes a day, 4 days a week for 26 weeks. It was used more often than not with students of low ability. In secondary-school studies the preponderance of uses was again mathematics. Of the 48 studies reviewed by Bangert-Drowns et al. (1985), 27 were in math, 11 in science, and the remaining 10 in a variety of different domains. The type of use was more varied than in elementary studies, with fairly even distribution across drill-and-practice, tutorial, CMI, and simulations. The average time spent on computers in secondary studies was the same as elementary: 26 hours distributed 20 minutes a day, 5 days a week for 26 weeks. The college studies were quite different; there was great variability on every dimension. Almost every subject is represented, with a very wide range of uses (59% tutorial and drill-and-practice, 13% CMI, and the remaining 28% simulations or programming). In the elementary studies, commercial software was used in 65% of the studies; in the college studies the percentage was only 17; at the college level, instructors were more likely to have written their own software. Also at the college level the computer was used with students of varying ability rather than just low achievers. In short, at the lower grades the reported studies of computer use were based largely on using the computer to help lower ability students with problems in mathematics. At the secondary-school level the preponderance of studies concerned mathematics, although there were more varied applications including tutoring and simulations. In college, the range of applications was very wide, ranging from short-term trivial drilling in facts to long-term tutoring for an entire course. Importantly, none of the meta-analyses describes in any detail the instructional programs under investigation. Studies that looked at CAI tutorials covering three particular concepts in biology are lumped together with CAI programs that provided a daily semester-long reinforcement opportunity for all the material in a course. With this as a backdrop, consider the findings.

Supplementing traditional instruction with CAI raises student achievement, especially in elementary schools. (The achievement findings are summarized in Table 4.2.) Meta-analyses show an average effect on measured achievement of 0.47 standard deviations in elementary school. This corresponds to the group taught with computers being ahead of their noncomputer counterparts by almost one-half school year in the outcomes measured. The equivalent figure for secondary-school students is 0.36 standard deviations, and for college students 0.29. The Kuliks (Kulik & Kulik, in press) feel that this declining effectiveness of CAI across grade levels reflects age-related differences in instructional needs. The learning task for most elementary students involves remembering facts and applying simple rules and formulas. These students profit from very structured drill-and-practice activities with instant feedback. College students, on the other hand, are responsible for a wider array of learning outcomes and are skilled at learning from a variety of instructional approaches; hence CAI does not show as distinct an advantage. But the Kulik conclusion does not fit with findings from the secondary-school studies showing that low-ability students achieved at an average of 0.46 standard deviations above their noncomputer classmates, mid-level students averaged 0.13, and high-ability students averaged 0.24 (Bangert-Drowns et al., 1985). Although there may be some merit to the Kulik hypothesis, it is likely that the advantage of CAI rests more with the instructional scope, sequence, and design of the particular CAI program or simulation. This type of information is rarely reported in the studies looked at by the meta-analysts.

There is agreement among the reviews that, where it was reported, the time it took to learn the subject matter was much less for computer-based instruction. (This applies only to the studies that reported the time taken to finish the course material, and that used CBI as a substitute for conventional classroom instruction. In some studies CBI was used to supplement classroom instruction, so it added to the time to learn.) In the college studies, the average time required to complete the computer-based unit of instruction was two-thirds that of the conventional instruction equivalent.

Other effects of computer-based instruction were noted in the reviews, none of them negative. In tests of retention several months

TABLE 4.2
Average Effect Sizes (Achievement) for Various Educational Groups
Taught by CAI, Simulations and CMI

Group	CAI	Simulations/Programming	CMI
Elementary[a]	.47	—	.07
Secondary[b]	.36	.07	.40
College[c]	.29	.23	.35
Adult[d]	.29	1.13	.72
Handicapped[e]	.59	—	—

NOTE: [a]Kulik, Kulik, & Bangert-Drowns (1985) [b]Bangert-Drowns et al. (1985) [c]Kulik & Kulik (in press) [d]Kulik, Kulik, & Schwalb (1986) [e]Schmidt, Weinstein, Niemic, & Walberg (in press).

after completion of the course there is a slight tendency for CBI students to exhibit more retention. Attitudes toward the subject matter and toward the quality of instruction in the two types of classes were not very different; what differences there were tended to favor computer-based instruction. CBI students were likely to have much more positive attitudes about computers.

There are not many studies in the area of computer simulations, especially at the elementary level. The effectiveness of using them, however, is summarized in the second column of Table 4.2. The few studies at the secondary level reported the CBI students doing about as well as those with conventional instruction. Simulations were somewhat more effective at the college level, and quite impressive in adult education.

Computer-managed instruction (CMI) presents a different application of electronic text. Here the computer is used primarily as a manager of instruction, testing for mastery and directing students to materials available in other media. In the research, this was rarely used at the elementary level, and then it showed no particular advantage (see Table 4.2, column 3). At the secondary and college level it is associated with higher achievement. A likely explanation for this is that CMI keeps better track of individual performance and can prescribe instruction more frequently than a teacher responsible for 30 to 150 students in a day.

Interestingly, Kulik, Bangert, and Williams (1983) report that findings in more recent studies show stronger effects of computer-based teaching on student achievement. They surmise that this is probably due to more appropriate use of instructional technology in recent years.

Considering all the studies where CBI was used, the weight of evidence shows a favorable outcome for CBI. What the studies do not show is whether this is due to the medium itself or the fact that the software prepared for the computer was much better designed than the classroom equivalent, with careful attention given to precise definitions, parsimonious explanations, and the application of instructional theory of the type discussed in chapter 1. In other words, the success of CBI may not be anything unique to the medium; rather the medium and technology associated with computer hardware and software design may motivate instructors to design lessons more carefully than is typically the case when they are preparing for daily classroom instruction.

This view is at the heart of a debate that has been ongoing in the literature for the last 3 years. Clark (1983) first put forth the notion that in most of the media studies (media of all types, not just electronic text) the difference between experimental and control students could just as easily be explained by the instructional program—the software—being delivered by the medium as by the medium itself. For example, Clark (1985) reviews most of the same studies included in the meta-analyses of Kulik and his colleagues just discussed. He found that in most studies there was no control for the amount of time spent in instruction; the CBI students usually received more instruction, and it is known that the more time students spend on the task the greater the likelihood that learning will occur. Clark also noted that most studies failed to insure that the same type of instruction was used in the computer and live instruction. In the few studies where it was controlled, the difference between the CBI group and the control averaged only 0.01 standard deviation units. Finally, Clark argues that a strong test of the unique contribution of CBI should be found in studies where the same teacher designed and delivered both the live and CBI instruction. In this situation we come closest to insuring that the instruction itself is the same, and only the computer is different. When Clark looked at these studies he found the average difference to favor CBI by 0.09 standard deviations—a small and non-significant difference.

If we accept Clark's argument we are still left with the conclusion that the computer can deliver well-designed instruction, and that it can do so repetitively. Although computers do have sick and "down" days like humans, the software does not. So the capacity of electronic text to deliver the best of human instruction (of the tutorial and drill-and-practice type) is established. And, to the extent students can work on the computer without the assistance of a teacher then the technology does offer something unique—it creates greater opportunity to individualize instruction for students and spread the teacher's skills more widely.

The Los Angeles Compensatory Education Study

It is useful to look at one carefully designed study with more detailed reporting on the instruction and the way in which it was used. A particularly difficult educational problem concerns students who are deficient in basic skills, and are relegated to compensatory education programs. Can the computer contribute to strengthening their skills? This is an important issue because the computer is being used extensively for this purpose in many inner-city school districts— especially those serving large numbers of minorities (Becker, 1984). In the late 1970s the Educational Testing Service (ETS) explored this issue with a 4-year study in The Los Angeles public schools (Ragosta, 1983). ETS found the most widely applicable drill-and-practice curricula in mathematics, reading, and language arts appropriate for Grades 1-6. The ones they chose were developed by Computer Curriculum Corporation (CCC) of Palo Alto, CA. They all operated on a minicomputer housed in each of the schools in the test site.

The math curriculum covered number concepts and the processes of addition, subtraction, multiplication, and division of whole numbers, fractions, decimals, and negative numbers. There were exercises appropriate to the full range of content and skill level for Grades 1-6. The reading curriculum was appropriate for only Grades 3-6. It contained exercises on word attack, vocabulary, literal comprehension, and work-study skills. The language curriculum was also for Grades 3-6. These exercises addressed principal parts, verb usage, subject-verb agreement, pronoun usage, contractions, possessives and negatives, modifiers, and sentence structure. In short, the three curricula covered a wide spectrum of topics that form the core of the elementary school curriculum.

According to need, students received 10-20 minutes per day of extra drill-and-practice in content areas in which they were having difficulty—10 minutes for math, 10 minutes for language arts and reading. After 1 year, CAI students in the math curriculum were compared with their classmates who did not receive computer drill (or any extra practice) in this content area. On curriculum-specific tests of computational skill they scored 0.80 standard deviation higher—a very large difference. On a standardized test of math computation (The California Test of Basic Skills [CTBS], computation subtest) they scored 0.36 standard deviation higher—smaller than the curriculum-specific tests, but equivalent to about a 4-month's edge. This advantage increased over the 3 years of the project, indicating that additional time on task resulted in superior computational performance. In the area of math concepts and applications, the results favored the CAI training, but the difference was quite small; but then the software did not include much content in these two domains.

The pattern in reading and language instruction is more complicated. After 1 year CAI students on the whole showed a modest advantage on the tests designed specifically to measure what the CAI programs taught—the advantage was smaller than for math. The advantage was minimal on the CTBS standardized tests. Several explanations are offered in the research report. All students received almost twice as much classroom time on language arts topics as math, so the computer training had less to offer that was unique. Second, there was a lot of variability in the performance of the various groups; some groups showed a very large advantage over their control groups, and others a very small one. This suggests that groups vary in their needs, and this in turn might vary by what is being taught in the students' regular classroom. A third point lies with the CAI programs themselves. The language arts and reading curricula were judged by some of the Los Angeles teachers to be insufficiently developed. There were insufficient exercises to challenge upper grade students; the students "topped out" on the tests of mastery early in the experiment. The researchers suggest that much better courseware is available today. (The CCC programs were those available in 1978.)

In short, the complex set of results provide ample evidence that CAI drill-and-practice courseware, when used repeatedly to reinforce basic skills in areas that are valued and tested for, can provide a valuable service in narrowing the gap of those students who are deficient. Its effectiveness depends on the quality of the software and its match with the educational goals of the curriculum, the availability of technology that can be easily accessed by students without disrupting the classroom management of on-going live instruction.

A small unreported study at the college level sheds additional light on the role of CBI. Dr. Lewis Kleinsmith teaches introductory biology at the University of Michigan. He has done so for the last 10 years. His class consists of three 1-hour lectures a week, supplemented by a textbook. Beginning in 1982 he began developing a tutorial computer program covering all of the concepts in the course. He soon required his students to work once a week on the tutorial in addition to the lectures. Beginning in 1976 he administered a multiple choice test for the course that he has used consistently for the last decade. Between 1977 and 1982, when students listened to lecture and studied traditionally, the average score for all students was 65%. Between 1983 and 1986 the average score was 74% — a full grade point higher. Importantly, he notes, the average score for minority students increased from 45% to 67%.

This study has some of the same confounding that Clark criticizes. In the course of developing the tutorial Kleinsmith could have improved his lectures, so the comparison is not valid. He also could have gotten smarter students in more recent years. But the most logical explanation is some mix of two factors. Kleinsmith wrote the tutorial, and in the course of doing this he had to think very carefully about the type of errors that students make in trying to understand the material. Probably, this influenced his lectures in a salutary way. But no matter how much the lectures improved it is unlikely that in a lecture he could give individualized attention to student difficulties in comprehension because these usually distribute themselves across different topics for different students. Finally, the tutorial provided additional required time-on-task that, Kleinsmith reports, the department could not provide in any other way. The money available for computers was not available to pay graduate student tutors to perform the same function.

Pogrow (personal communication, May, 1986) reviewed a number of the same studies as Kulik and Clark, but also looked at a major one in Arkansas that has not yet been reported in the literature. He argues that CAI offers an advantage to the extent the CAI is automated. The CCC curriculum is an example of automated software. The curriculum is established and self-diagnosing of student difficulties. It does not require interventions by the teacher to determine a student's deficiencies nor to choose the particular piece of drill-and-practice software appropriate to the deficiency.

Ragosta reports that the costs of the somewhat-expensive prototype program in Los Angeles were well within the normal expenditures for compensatory education students. But is it cost-effective? The research results were critiqued from the perspective of the cost-benefits of computer-based remedial training compared with other interventions such as reduction in class size, peer tutoring, instructional television, teacher training, and electronic calculators. Although there is some controversy over the appropriate way to measure costs and benefits (Levin, Glass, & Meister, 1984; Niemic, Blackwell, & Walberg, 1986) the most compelling evidence to this author favors CAI as the most cost-effective—perhaps by a margin as big as 2-to-1—over peer tutoring, the next most effective intervention.

PLATO and TICCIT

In a category by themselves are the tutoring products developed on large mainframe computers for use by distant learners. The most notable of these is the PLATO system developed by the University of Illinois and Control Data Corporation. The PLATO library contains over 12,000 hours of instruction in basic skills, technical training, and higher education. The major design of the programs is traditional tutorial, with instructional frames followed by mastery tests and conditional branching. The system is used by learners working at computer terminals located around the country in factories and stand-alone learning centers. PLATO's primary use to date has been for in-service training in industry. United Airlines uses PLATO to bring new trainees up to the entry level for transitional training. Yearly, Control Data Corporation—the hardware developer for PLATO—trains about 7,000 programmers, operators, and technicians for the computer industry. The Navy trains large numbers of recruits in basic skills using the system. College use of the system has been for courses in developmental English, physics, electrical engineering, accounting, educational psychology, and astronomy. Like the drill-and-practice software for microcomputers, PLATO courses are designed to supplement classroom instruction. But the PLATO courses are more comprehensive in their coverage of course material than most instructional software developed for microcomputers.

With such extensive course development, and with so many courses as part of the system, one would expect its use to be associated with high achievement. But very few studies have been reported in the literature; most of what there is does not support this expectation. Students who take this type of instruction have little advantage. When cost is taken into account, the military has concluded that

PLATO is less cost-effective than noncomputerized, individualized instruction (Office of Technology Assessment, 1982).

TICCIT was developed at Brigham Young University in the early 1970s. It uses a more sophisticated technology than PLATO. It is designed to integrate television with minicomputers to create complete stand-alone CAI courses. The software gives the learner much more control over the selection of instructional components and pacing than does PLATO. For example, the learner can choose the instructional unit to work on, repeat it, and call for as many examples as desired, alter the level of difficulty, ask for a quiz, or move on to a new unit at any time. A new wrinkle being added is "intelligent advisement," whereby a learner is advised if she or he is pursuing an inefficient learning strategy.

Reports on TICCIT's instructional effectiveness underscore some limitations. In one report (Bunderson, 1975), students receiving instruction solely on the TICCIT system performed equal to the students who received the instruction in a conventional classroom. This suggests that well-designed CAI can even teach as a stand-alone device replacing the teacher. But the same research notes that TICCIT students were much less likely to complete the course. This finding underscores the difficulty of using CBI to completely replace a teacher. At present, in our culture, the supervision and stimulation of a human teacher is still an important ingredient for most students.

Business and Industrial Training

One might predict that business and industry would be the most likely users of computer-based instruction. Unlike schools that have a regular captive audience proceeding through a curriculum in a fixed geographical location, business is frequently faced with training small groups on a needs basis, often at a location other than a central office. Having a stand-alone capability in computer-based instruction would seem a logical solution to this educational problem. Indeed, as was mentioned in the discussion of PLATO, computer-based training has been found to be somewhat effective for two types of education. One is providing basic-skills training associated with proficiency at high-school level courses in reading, writing, and math. A second is providing training in skills such as computer programming where the skill to be acquired is computer-based.

A recent report by the Office of Technology Assessment (OTA;

1982) indicates that there are real limitations of the computer for many educational needs in business:

> Computer-assisted instruction has, to date, been found to be of little value in advanced engineering and software development courses, as well as in apprenticeship skills training. This is due to the complexity of the information that must be conveyed and, in the case of apprenticeship, to the need for repeated demonstration by a knowledgeable instructor who can respond to a trainee's questions and who can demonstrate on actual equipment. Many corporate trainers still feel that classroom instruction is the best approach. Others resist the use of technology in their programs because they feel that they are often being sold technology for technology's sake, rather than as a tool to be utilized within the framework of an existing instructional system. (p. 103)

Insights into this apparent resistance to using computer-based instruction was provided by an individual who trains instructional designers for industry. She noted that computer-based instruction requires very sophisticated task analysis and branching design. Most of the industrial trainers who come to this person's training workshops are instructors whose primary strength lies in their ability to develop organized lesson plans and then deliver instruction following that plan. They are not trained in instructional theory and are not sufficiently skilled to do the necessary computer-based development. The strength of their supervisors is in management, so they cannot provide the necessary expertise either.

The assessment in the OTA report highlights a particular problem with the electronic text medium. Electronic text, even when supplemented with graphics, is inadequate to show sufficient detail to train certain types of workers in the intricacies of the objects or machines with which they will be working. The lack of the right type of feedback is also a limitation. Training apprentices often requires that the learner see and manipulate a device, and then receive feedback on the manipulation. Learning to label parts of an object requires high-resolution pictures. The next chapter discusses how developers are merging electronic text and graphics with audio and video in an attempt to overcome some of these limitations.

New Trends in CAI

There are important trends occurring in the CAI arena that promise to change the very character of CAI in the near future. They reflect the influence of developments in the field of expert systems and artificial intelligence. The traditional CAI program is a series of lessons comprised of three components: (a) instructional frames that present new concepts; (b) inquisitory frames that test for understanding of the concept. The student's responses result in either a continuation of the lesson (when the correct response is given) or in branching to one or more; and (c) remedial frames that explain the concept in a different way. For the student receiving the remedial material another inquisitory frame tests for mastery and the results determine whether to return the student to the main lesson or continue with remediation.

For the most part, this strategy is linear. Comprehension is tested at a number of nodes along a sequential presentation of information, and remediation takes into account only the immediate misunderstanding. What is missing is an analysis of the learners' pattern of thinking that might be obtained by looking across a series of responses. Very ambitious efforts are being made in this area from two different viewpoints. The field of expert systems and artificial intelligence is developing sophisticated computer algorithms that analyze the match between the learner's strategy for solving a problem and the strategy used by experts in that field. For example, John Seeley Brown developed *BUGGY* as a program that detects the nature of the errors a learner is making in subtraction problems. If the student is going about the process wrong (subtracting from left to right or failing to borrow) she or he is redirected to correct the very process used to subtract, rather than just being told she or he is wrong. Systems being developed to fulfill this analytic function are only in the prototype stage at present. They require sophisticated input devices (e.g., bit-mapped touch screens that can detect whether the learner first manipulates the units or tens digit in a subtraction problem), enormous amounts of computing power, and the patience to develop a very large database that represents how experts solve problems. At present, the most extensive work is being done in disciplines such as mathematics that are organized very tightly around unambiguous and inviolable rules.

Another group is approaching the same problem from a different perspective. These are the instructional product developers such as David Merrill (and Joseph Scandura, Bob Tennyson, and Charles Reigeluth) who have spent many years refining the basic tutorial model just described. These developers are trying to add what they call *intelligent advisement* to their programs based on an analysis of the pattern of responses to several questions that suggest that the learner is pursuing the wrong learning strategy. This approach requires much less computing power and is more likely to appear in regularly available programs in the near future.

Interactive Simulations

The traditional tutorial model has been applied to the teaching of verbal information (names, facts); concepts (the definition and examples of temperature, democracy, weight, etc.); and procedural rules and relations (multiplication of 2-digit numbers, applying heat to a solution increases molecular activity, the presence of a larger-than-usual number of white cells in the blood is a sign of infection). A particular instructional problem arises in teaching about complex systems of any kind when many procedural rules interact in the operation of the system, and the interrelationship is itself complicated. Consider teaching medical students to detect the presence of illness in the human body. The body is an organism governed by many systems. Various external symptoms are clues to its well-being (average operating temperature, pulse, skin color, white cells in the blood, sugar level in the urine). The meaning of measurements of each of these indicators is taught as a particular procedural rule. (Body temperature in one range is normal, in another range abnormal and a clue that one of many different types of infection may be present.) Ultimately, a medical student needs to be taught not a collection of discrete procedural rules; rather, how certain constellations of symptoms are to be interpreted. The computer has the ability to simulate complex systems such as the human body and to allow students to discover for themselves the interrelationships without actually working on the live organism. This is done in a simulation from Ohio State University called *CASE: Computer-Aided Simulation of Clinical Encounter*. Medical students sit at a terminal and they are presented with 1 of 20 patients. They know nothing about the patient when they start. They ask the patient (in natural language typed on the terminal keyboard) what is bothering him or her, so they have the practice of asking for the appropriate patient symptoms. They are not told any more information than they ask for. The student can request various laboratory tests to get internal indicators of health. Finally, they must recommend a treatment regimen and medication. On each of these activities they are graded on the basis of expert judgment (that of a panel of doctors who made the simulation) as to what information should have been obtained from the patient, what the symptoms indicate in terms of illness, and what the appropriate treatment regimen should be. This represents one of the most complex of simulations now available.

There are other simulations that are less complex, and that require the learner to integrate less knowledge. In *Sir Isaac Newton's Games* from Sunburst, students have the opportunity to test their knowledge of the various complex formulas that govern motion. The catalog (Sunburst, 1986) describes the activities in this way. "Students begin by trying to move an object around a track. They must determine whether to kick the object or let it coast. The track can be placed on earth (on either ice, sand, or grass) or near the sun or out in space. The effect on motion of each of the environments can then be studied" (The Best from Sunburst, 1986, p. 7).

There are a number of simulations that deal not with known rules from science or math or some other discipline, but rather they deal with general problem-solving skills by presenting environments that have rules that can be either discovered or made up. Games such as *Gertrude's Secrets* and *Rocky's Boots* from The Learning Company provide mind-expanding challenges to developing rules to control the actions of various games. All of these programs make extensive use of the graphics capabilities of computers. At this point, their educational potential has not been systematically studied and reported in the literature. An exception is a study by Dalbey, Tourniaire, and Linn (n.d.). The authors report that a 3-week course based on *Rocky's Boots* taught students a variety of problem-solving skills.

The value of the content-oriented simulations needs to be studied, but they present a particular problem. Often, the outcomes for which they are designed reflect outcomes that have never been part of a course goal. The patient simulation represents a set of learning goals that had never been part of a paper-and-pencil exam before; it was only part of the clinical evaluation made of advanced students. Similarly, with the *Isaac Newton* simulation—physics students often are evaluated on their knowledge of the effect of a single variable (e.g., gravity or friction) on an object in motion, but rarely are they evaluated on their understanding of the interrelationship of the various laws of motion. Traditional studies that compare computer and noncomputer groups might not show differences on standardized tests of knowledge in various domains. They must be specially tailored to the type of knowledge being taught by simulations.

Programming: Does it Increase Problem-Solving Skills?

One of the most tantalizing claims for electronic text relates to teaching children higher order problem-solving skills using the very tools that create the medium. These skills, it is argued, should emerge as by-products of teaching students how to analyze a computer-soluble problem, and then write and debug a program to solve the problem. This idea has been put forth by many people, but none so persuasively as Seymour Papert (1980), the creator of the programming language Logo:

> I began to see how children who had learned to program computers could use very concrete computer models to think about thinking and to learn about learning and in doing so, enhance their powers as epistemologists. . . . Learning to be a master programmer is learning to become highly skilled at isolating and correcting "bugs," the parts that keep the program from working. The question to ask about the program is not whether it is right or wrong, but if it is fixable. If this way of looking at intellectual products were generalized to how the larger culture thinks about knowledge and its acquisition, we all might be less intimidated by our fears of "being wrong." (p. 23)

The notion, then, is that programming approximates many cognitively demanding tasks in life. As Nickerson (cited in Pea & Kurland, 1984a) notes:

> It is a creative endeavor requiring planning, precision in the use of language, the generation and testing of hypotheses, the ability to identify action sequences that will realize specified objectives, careful attention to detail, and a variety of other skills that seem to reflect what thinking is all about. (p. 2)

Research on these claims began a few years ago and the findings are just now coming in; the results are mixed. Pea and Kurland (1984c) point out the complexity of defining the concept "problem-solving skills." It is clear from a long line of research on the development of such skills that they tend to be task-specific and usually do not generalize across domains. To test the ability of programming to nurture these skills Pea and Kurland used 32 third- to sixth-grade students. Half of the group had 30 hours of Logo instruction spread across 4 months; the other half had no instruction. At the end of 4 months students were given a planning task in which they had to decide the most efficient way to accomplish a number of classroom chores. From this study and a replication, Pea and Kurland (1984) conclude the following:

> At a minimum, what we have demonstrated is that the strong claims for generalizable cognitive benefits from learning to program in Logo with the discovery learning pedagogy need serious reexamination. In spite of the fact that our studies were conducted in relatively computer-rich classrooms—with one computer for each four students . . . we did not observe the predicted cognitive benefits of greater planning skills in students learning Logo programming. (p. 44)

Using 18 six-year-old children in the first grade, Clements and Gullo (1984) did find measurable effects after a 12-week class in Logo programming. These children showed more divergent thinking and were more reflective in analyzing a discrimination problem. They could also give clearer directions to a friend about how to follow a map. But the number of students in this study is quite small and the teachers gave them quite a bit of guidance, suggesting that Logo itself may not have been responsible.

The task of developing problem-solving skills in learners is complex. It seems likely that if computer programming is going to contribute to this development it must entail (a) students acquiring extensive experience with programming—perhaps four semesters, and (b) they must be taught by a teacher who helps learners reflect on the general strategies that they apply to "debugging" problems (Johnston, Luker, & Mergendoller, 1984; Linn, 1985). Whether computer programming is the new Latin—as Pea has dubbed the enthusiastic reception accorded programming—is still an open question.

Patterson and Smith (1986) approach the question of computers and problem solving from the opposite direction. They ask, what are the elements of problem-solving skills, and with which of these can the computer help? They start with a definition of *higher order thinking* as active, sustained cognitive effort directed at solving a complex problem using prior knowledge and experience in addressing the problem. From this definition, they inquire as to what are the skills required to engage successfully in this type of thinking. They list the following: (a) knowledge of facts and rules at the "automatic" level (readily accessible, on the tip of the tongue); (b) the development of schema to better organize and remember new knowledge; (c) knowledge of heuristics appropriate to the task; and (d) ample opportunities to practice problem solving and be successful at it.

To enhance abilities in each of these skill areas they enumerate different types of computer activities and specific programs. In other words, they recognize that higher order thinking skills are the result of articulated instruction of various sorts. They also make it clear that although various computer-based activities can reasonably contribute to development of skills in this area, it is still an instructional task that requires a knowledgeable teacher to orchestrate the activities and guide the thought processes of students.

INSTRUMENTAL APPLICATIONS:
COMPUTERS AS TOOLS

Computer tools are programs designed to enhance users' capabilities to manage information. Many of them have distinctly educational applications. The most obvious tool is the word processor. This allows a user to enter text using a computer keyboard and to have the computer manipulate the words in several useful ways. It can format the words so the text appears neat; it can electronically erase, add, and reorder words, making copyediting and revision easy. With the addition of analytic software the computer can check for spelling and syntactical errors; it can even assess characteristics of text such as sentence length and word size, responding with suggestions for shorter sentences or simpler words. It has been argued that these capabilities can contribute to the quality of composition of learners in three ways. Planners (*Think Tank* or *Quill*) can help writers organize their thoughts to be more persuasive and logical. The word processor allows for easier entry and revision, and should make writers more verbose and potentially more descriptive. By taking advantage of various textual analysis programs, learners should be able to identify technical problems more easily and, with revision being so easy, produce technically better papers.

An example of an integrated package of planning and processing tools is *Quill.* It is a microcomputer-based package of programs for young writers. It was specifically designed with elementary school children in mind. The set of programs includes a planner that asks the user what kind of report she or he is writing, and then asks salient questions to guide idea development. If the report is to be a book report, the program queries for the title of the book, the authors, the main characters, the story line, and the reader's evaluation. The planner is connected to a word processor. Other components include a library for storing text, a publisher for formatting finished text, and story maker, a story construction tool.

Research to date on *Quill* is quite limited. Based on pilot tests, Rubin and Bruce (in press) suggest that the program extends a teacher's guidance of the writing process by helping students structure their writing. Although it facilitates copyediting, without active intervention by teachers it does not teach students how to revise text (Bruce & Rubin, 1985).

An interesting side effect was noted by the developers of *Quill*. With only one or two computers in most classrooms, students would get in line to use the machine. While waiting, they would often look over each other's draft, an activity rarely encouraged in most classrooms where text is being written. Yet, many educators feel that peer critique is a good technique for the development of good writing. The computer program indirectly facilitated a useful classroom practice.

Research on the general set of issues surrounding computers and writing has just begun. Scardamalia and Bereiter (1985) and Pintrich, Cross, Kozma, and McKeachie (1985) summarize the available research. They note that computers have been shown to improve the surface features of a paper (spelling, grammar, format, etc.), although this was established in research that used very sophisticated programs such as *Writer's Workbench,* as opposed to the type of off-the-shelf software available to most authors. The simple use of a word processor instead of a paper-and-pencil has not been shown to improve the internal and higher order aspects of students' writing such as the organization or the rhetorical quality. Although the word processor may make it easier to enter and revise text, it does not of itself guide a writer to select and organize the elements of persuasive well-organized thinking and writing.

Another computer tool generating some interest is the database manager. It is being applied in two different ways in education, one of which is as an aid in teaching the processes of science. Science is often taught as the memorization of facts, principles, and generalizations. Discovery is reserved for laboratory sessions, and most laboratory exercises are set up to lead a student to certain conclusions. But the practice of science is something different; it entails a search for new meaning in raw data. To teach this process, data can be entered into a computerized database and students can manipulate the data to draw conclusions for themselves with the guidance of a teacher. This idea has been encouraged by some educators, but it has not been studied. Because it represents teaching science in an entirely different fashion from the way science teachers were trained, it may not receive widespread use. In the 1960s and 1970s the process-approach to science teaching was advocated by various national science groups. After a decade of experimentation, the process approach was judged too difficult to implement in the typical classroom.

A second use of a database manager is similar to drill-and-practice. Using a visual-based manager such as *Filevision,* descriptive text about an object (or a process that can be visualized) is stored in the database and linked to elements in a graphical display of the object. For example, an anatomy lesson might have a graphical representation of an eye showing the iris, pupil, cornea, and various muscles and nerves. By pointing to any of these parts with the computer's cursor, the learner can retrieve the text that explains what it is. The learner is in control of the information needed to memorize the salient labels for the object's parts. In this application the computer is being used as a drill-and-practice tutor. Such applications have not been evaluated at this point.

INFORMATIONAL APPLICATIONS: RETRIEVAL AND EXCHANGE

An intriguing set of applications for electronic text arise out of the capabilities inherent in electronic text technologies for storing information and retrieving it from distant locations. One such application is accessing databases of bibliographic information such as one of the 200 databases in the DIALOG system that provide abstracts and citations on a wide range of topics. The card catalogs of some libraries have been made available on-line so users with a computer and modem can find out from their workplace whether a book is carried by the library without having to go there. The ability to alter the database instantly is a useful characteristic in applications such as these where the information is constantly changing as new publications become available.

A related application is the exchange of electronic text between people either through message systems or computer conferences. Because of the incompatibility of people's schedules, this is a serious limitation in the utility of the telephone for communication. Computer-based message systems and bulletin boards allow individuals to exchange messages or broadcast bulletins in delayed or asynchronous time. In these applications the computer serves as an electronic mailbox that can be accessed to send or receive messages at a time convenient to each mailbox owner. Such systems are being used increasingly in business. They are beginning to be used in education as well on a number of computer-intensive campuses, but usually as one capability within a more complicated computer conference system. Most of the research on message systems has been done in business settings (see Rice, 1984, for a review of this research.)

A computer conference (CC) consists of a host computer to which members of a group connect using terminals. In synchronous conferences members of the group exchange ideas in real time, using text and graphics to communicate. In asynchronous conferences the group shares ideas by typing into filespace that is shared by all members. Whenever a conference member connects with the computer she or he finds an item or issue to be discussed and the record of other members' responses to the item. If the member has something to add it is automatically inserted at the end of the discussion record. In this way, a group discussion is carried on entirely in delayed time.

Synchronous Computer Conferencing.   This form of CC is used for a special kind of long-distance teaching. It is an application of a new technology to an old problem (see chapter 2) — providing specialized instruction to small isolated groups. For example, many rural schools are unable to provide advanced courses, because their student body is too small to justify the costs. As a solution, experiments are currently going on in which a course such as advanced calculus is taught by a single teacher to a class of 15 students where the students are located in groups of 1–3 in a number of geographically separate rural schools. A telephone conference call serves to connect the students and teacher for oral communication; networked microcomputers serve as a two-way electronic blackboard. Here is a description of its application in a high-school calculus course as described by Perlez (1985):

> The IBM PC [in each school] is equipped with a writing tablet that allows [students and the teacher] to write on the screen and their notations can be seen in every other location. A cordless microphone and a speaker phone sit beside the computer. Professor Tucker was

talking the other day about downward curves, second derivatives and solutions to a written problem. The students could see Professor Tucker's equations emerge on the screen as he wrote.

"I'd like someone to draw for me," Professor Tucker said as he finished his part of the problem. Let's go to Mount Upton." Seventy miles away from Oxford, one of the three calculus students at Mount Upton High School drew an upward curving line. There were murmurs of approval in Oxford among the four students in Patrick's class as a line, sketched correctly, emerged on their screen. (p. 19)

Such programs are experimental at present. The success of the aforementioned program will be judged by the students' performance on the Advanced Placement calculus test of the College Board exam. But there is no reason to think such a program should not work. The medium and technology are being used quite obviously as a simple extension of the classroom over time and space. The medium itself is not providing anything that the instructor or students would not provide in face-to-face instruction.

Asynchronous Computer Conferencing.   This type of conference is being used experimentally in higher education on a number of computer-intensive campuses. It is used to extend classroom discussion of issues, and thus extends the amount of time on task. Following is an example taken from a graduate course in electronic learning. It illustrates the use of an a so-called item (here inserted by the course instructor) and a series of responses generated by students and the instructor.

Item 9: Jan 23, 10:13am, 4 lines, 21 responses
Author: [The Instructor]
Topic: Efficiency across the curriculum

Computer-based learning promises to make learning more efficient; students will not need as much time to learn the same material. But society is not well served by helping students complete their learning sooner than their age-mates. Agree or disagree?

9:1 [item 9, response 1]. (Jan 24, 10:25am). [Student 1]: I can give the same example I gave in class. There is a relatively standard linear algebra course taken by college students in many fields, including math, computer science, biology, and economics. Most students hate the course, because it very tediously teaches manipulative skills that can be done more accurately on a computer. If the computer was used as a linear algebra tool, and students did not need to learn how to solve equations manually, they could easily move through this preliminary material and spend more time where it is really needed—on the difficult concepts of linearity and vector spaces, on important applications to mathematical modeling (Markov chains, graph theory, etc.), and differential equations. In this example students would not complete their courses sooner; the course would change to cover different material in the same period of time.

* * *

9:6. (Jan 28/86, 11:05am). [Student 2]: . . . there are always students that are bored and slowed by traditional classroom education and would both enjoy and benefit from an opportunity to move faster with the help of a technologically based program.

9:7. (Jan 29/86, 9:15am). [Instructor]: Suppose you speed up some students, how do you handle them within the current system that assigns students to one grade between September and June, and keeps them in school through at least age 16?

* * *

9:13. (Jan 30/86, 10:13pm). [Student 3]: At this point, I am not going to try to address the technical problems of coordinating ability groups and moving students through K-12 at their own pace, but I am going to address the questions of whether such a fluid system would be desirable . . .

This excerpt from an actual class conference illustrates how a conference can be used to extend the class discussion of issues germane to the content of the course. The computer is an enabling technology, permitting modest reorganization of the classroom structure to allow more opportunity for discussion. Little research has been performed in this arena. There are many issues to be explored, including the effects of impersonal communication on communication style, time use patterns of students and faculty, and the communication problems (channel capacity, information "chunking") associated with interchanges in a new medium—the characteristics of which are somewhere between oral discourse and short essays. Asynchronous CC holds the promise of enhancing the support available for the distant learner, but also the student on a campus where access to classmates and faculty is limited by the lengthy time usually required for a formal appointment and meeting.

THE MEDIUM AND TECHNOLOGY

Kulik and his colleagues have performed meta-analyses of several different instructional technologies, including audio-tutorial (Kulik et al., 1979a), Keller's Personalized System of Instruction (Kulik, et al., 1979b), and print-based programmed instruction (Kulik, Cohen, & Ebeling, 1980a). In looking across all of these studies, Kulik and Bangert-Drowns (1983) conclude:

> [Print based] programmed instruction and individualized instruction have had only limited success in raising student achievement or improving student attitude in precollege education. Computer-based instruction, on the other hand, has raised student achievement significantly in numerous studies, dramatically affected the amount of time needed for teaching and learning, and greatly altered student attitudes toward the computer. (p. 156)

There is compelling evidence across hundreds of studies that something called *computer-based instruction* is a useful approach for learning and instruction. Having concluded this, we know little at this point about the characteristics of electronic text programming that are responsible for such an optimistic assessment. The most obvious candidates are the ability of the computer program to provide immediate feedback on achievement, reinforce correct answers (a smiling icon or an encouraging text), and provide remedial material for incorrect answers. In the course of doing this it can efficiently provide each learner with the unique material he or she needs at the time, unlike a lecture or textbook that is built around instructor expectations about what a group—on the average—needs to know. The instructional task can be accomplished in a context that is private. Finally, the delivery device—the flickering text under the command of the user—is inherently captivating (Lepper & Malone, in press; Malone, 1980). But as with video, the success of computer-based instruction rests more with the design of the instructional programs than it does with the medium itself.

Chapter 5 _____

A Hybrid Medium: Integrated Videodiscs

Recent developments of inexpensive microcomputers, high-resolution monitors, and sophisticated computer software has brought flexible, interactive text within the reach of a wide range of teachers, parents, and industrial trainers. This is a great advance over the teaching machines and computer-assisted instruction of the 1960s, and a giant step toward self-contained electronic instruction. But the ability of the best computer software to emulate a teacher is limited in ways discussed in chapter 4. An important limitation is the inability to provide visual information that corresponds to the programmed instruction. Instruction in some topic areas absolutely requires imagery; other areas are enhanced by it. Both still and moving images are necessary adjuncts to instruction in the physical sciences and in technical training in business and industry. The teaching of social sciences is enhanced by moving images (movies) of social phenomena such as Congress in action, delinquent gangs, or daily life in faraway lands. Social aspects of business, such as sales techniques, are more easily taught if audiovisual sequences of typical customer behavior can be shown to learners.

The potential to marry electronic text and graphics with video was made possible by the development of the videodisc and related technology that provides an interface between the videodisc and microcomputer. Although these developments are quite recent, they have captured the imagination of many persons in industrial training and, to a lesser extent, people in higher education. Experimental software is just now being developed for secondary education. The videodisc is novel, expensive, and only recently evaluated for its educational potential.

THE WORKINGS OF THE INTEGRATED VIDEODISC

A videodisc resembles a long-playing phonograph record. One side of a disc can hold 54,000 frames, either pictures or pages of text, along with an accompanying audio track. Each frame has a numerical address and can be retrieved and displayed on a television or video monitor. The visual image and audio track are stored in billions of microscopic pits on the disc. A videodisc player translates these pits to sound and pictures by means of a laser beam that is focused on the surface of the disc. In contrast to film or videotape, the disc is close to indestructible. The pictures are of very high quality and retrievable from anywhere on the disc within 1 second. Retrieval is at the command of a user or a computer program, as either a still frame or pictures in motion. The still frame looks much like a 35mm slide, without the distortion associated with freeze-action of a videotape. Motion sequences are equivalent to those of videotape.

A videodisc player contains the laser beam and translation hardware. A separate television or video monitor provides sight and sound. The player contains manual controls to specify a single frame or sequence of frames to be shown. Frame selection can also be controlled by electronic impulses emanating from a microcomputer. By itself a videodisc and associated player is a very sophisticated audio-visual device, allowing the advantage over other linear video technologies of fast random access to material. Additional devices are required to provide the most intriguing instructional capacities.

A microcomputer with instructional software can be attached directly to the player and used to specify which visuals are to be selected from the disc. An overlay circuit card and high-resolution graphics card in the microcomputer superimposes computer text and graphics on the video so a single display monitor can be used for both. Beyond this, courseware in the microcomputer provides the interactive part of the instruction. It is written in a way that calls for video on the disc at appropriate times. Here is a sequence that might typify use of a videodisc and micro in tandem: In a lesson on carburetor repair the computer provides text, asking the learner what aspects of carburetor repair he or she wants to study. In response to directions typed on the computer keyboard, a videodisc segment is shown on the monitor that points out the salient physical features of the carburetor and goes through the necessary sequence of steps to adjust it for particular malfunctions. The learner can control the pace of presentation or even stop the presentation to study a visual for a longer time than programmed.

As with all computer-assisted instruction, a distinguishing feature is the inclusion in the computer software of diagnostic and remediation loops. Authors design the courseware to query learners frequently about their understanding of the material presented. This information is used to control the videodisc presentation. When a learner's response to a query suggests misunderstanding, a prior sequence of instruction is repeated, or a new sequence of instruction is activated that explains the material in a different way. Learner responses can also be used to verify mastery or to control the pace of instruction. This integrated instructional system attempts to mimic a tutorial situation. An important key to success is building into the courseware effective and believable responses to every possible learner difficulty.

Various peripherals open up additional possibilities. A touch-sensitive screen on the TV monitor permits the learner to respond by simply touching it rather than through use of the more intimidating computer keyboard. Light pens can also be used as a source of learner input. In the carburetor repair example taken from an existing Ford Motor Company training program, the mechanic uses a light pen to simulate the steps he would take with a vacuum gauge and screwdriver to adjust the carburetor. Voice input is available as well, although the current recognizable vocabulary is limited. A voice synthesizer and sound generator that provide both variety and flexibility are on the output side. The most novel peripheral is a simulator that approximates motion. At American Airlines, a pilot trainer can simulate takeoffs, landings, and abnormal responses of the plane. Pilots can practice their flight procedures and "feel" the results of their adjustments in a very realistic way. The motions are coordinated with visuals stored on the videodisc.

Videodisc instruction is very expensive. The cost of videodisc courseware—the visuals on disc—ranges from $35,000 to $100,000 per hour. This is similar to the cost of producing film or videotape, because it requires a production crew and cast. In fact, all of the visual material is first produced on film or videotape and transferred to disc only when it is judged perfect. Like a phonograph record, a disc is a read-only device and cannot be modified once it is pressed. The cost of the associated computer courseware which drives the videodisc ranges from $2,000 to $20,000 per hour of instructional video material. The cost of the disc mastering is less than $10,000. Once a master is made, copy costs depend on volume. At volumes more than 500, the cost is less than $50. In addition to the disc, consumers need hardware to use it. At the least, it costs $5,000 for a videodisc player, monitor, microcomputer, and special circuit boards. An integrated version of the hardware complete with a touch screen costs closer to $20,000.

It is extremely difficult to create good courseware. Because videodisc instruction is trying to supplant the teacher completely, it must be extremely sophisticated. It is clear from the discussion in chapter 1 that human teachers constantly make very complex instructional decisions based on both impressionistic and formally measured assessments of student needs. Responding to subtle cues from students, a teacher judges when it is time to test for mastery or alter the planned presentation to make it somewhat simpler (or more complex), or make the instructional activity more motivating. The teacher frequently singles out certain students for remedial work in a prerequisite skill. All of these judgments, and the appropriate responses, must be built into the courseware. Yet, once a master is made, the videodisc courseware is unchangeable; and although the computer courseware can be altered, doing so defeats the purpose of an instructional tool designed to free learners from an instructor.

AVAILABLE COURSEWARE

There are many more videodisc courses available for business and industry than for schools. In situations where there is frequent change in the product or high turnover in the work force, integrated videodisc instruction is being turned to as a more cost effective means of training workers than face-to-face instruction. Most of the courses are very recent—completed in 1983 and 1984—and most cover technical skills for company employees. Examples include: Ford Motor Company, carburetor repair; General Electric, repair of jet and diesel engines; Digital Equipment Corporation, computer repair; AT&T, installation and maintenance of new phone products; American Airlines, pilot training; Maritime Institute of Technology, mariner pilot training; Sizzler, taking customer orders for food; J. C. Penney, inventory control; Xerox, sales techniques; Florida Department of Health, determination of eligibility for benefits under Aid to Families with Dependent Children.

Unlike the training sector in business and industry, the education community has not perceived as great a need for the integrated videodisc instructional system. A few discs have been produced experimentally. With funding from the Annenberg/CPB Project, the University of Nebraska produced six experimental videodiscs to simulate several science laboratory experiments on the topics of titration, respiration, chemical decision making, physics in motion, climate and life, and energy transformation (Davis, 1984). These discs simulate the laboratory experiment. "In these simulated science labs, students use a microcomputer and video screen the way they use test tubes, lab equipment, or chemicals in a traditional lab. Electronically, they mix chemicals, modify temperatures, and then observe the results" (Davis, 1984, p. 1). At WICAT in Orem, UT several discs have been developed to teach Spanish as a second language (Williams, Quinn, & Gale, 1983). In these lessons, a learner is presented a setting or context with Spanish being spoken. The learner is given opportunities to hear the language properly spoken, look for visual cues, and then practice it. The lessons do not provide a critique of learner responses, but it is interactive at points. The learner gets to choose which Spanish response is the correct one for the situation, and the videodisc continues according to the selection. Other applications are described by DeBloois, Maki, and Hall (1984).

EVALUATION OF THE INTEGRATED VIDEODISC

At this point in time, there are only a few examples of formal evaluation of videodisc instruction. Two are discussed here: one for academic applications and another for industrial training.

Academic Applications

Barbara Davis took the science lab videodiscs to seven different universities and colleges across the country where she secured cooperation to try them on a voluntary basis in appropriate courses.

Although the test of effectiveness was not as tight as might be desired, the novelty of the intervention made rigorous assessment impossible. Nonetheless, the evaluation was most enlightening. Davis (1984) lists a number of advantages to videodisc for simulating laboratory experiments. One of these is time savings (Davis, 1984):

> During a conventional lab, students spend time setting up, waiting between data collection points, cleaning up, correcting errors, and so on. With a videodisc, the experiments can move more rapidly. For example, in [the Respiration Lab videodisc] students need not wait for the temperature changes but can see results almost instantly. Students who spent 40 minutes in the videodisc Respiration labs were able to carry out a complete experiment of one organism at three temperatures. In a traditional lab this might take up to three hours. (p. 3)

Another advantage related to clarity of procedures.

> Students using the videodiscs appear less confused about what to do than students in the traditional lab who frequently check with the teaching assistant to make sure the experiment is being conducted accurately. The videodisc medium provides a more structured and individualized approach than most traditional labs. Interactive preparation is obligatory since students must work through introductory sections before conducting the experiment. In contrast, in traditional lab, preparation tends to be left to students with mixed results, or delivered as a prelab lecture during which students can remain passive or inattentive. In the traditional lab with one TA and 20–30 students, students receive less individual monitoring and tutorial assistance. As a result students cannot always receive timely clarification or correction. (p. 4)

Another advantage noted by Davis is the fact that integrated videodisc instruction necessitates active student learning—something that is not required in face-to-face instruction other than in the tutorial mode. Davis reports that students like the self-pacing, the user control, immediate feedback, and the consistency of presentation. They also report learning a lot. In a few selected tests comparing the results of this type of instruction with that of classmates in the traditional lab at the same school, the scores of the videodisc students were equal to or greater than those of the traditional lab students.

On the negative side of the ledger, Davis noted a number of things. Some of these are inherent in the medium; others are a function of the inexperience of developers and the current limitations of hardware. She found a number of weaknesses in both hardware and software. The following is an enumeration of the problems. Frequently, the computer software contained bad loops from which a learner could not escape; in some cases the software directed learners to inappropriate remediation loops. Often the image resolution was insufficient for fine detail. The hardware broke down. Because this kind of simulated lab was unique at the test colleges, there was no one around to assist when difficulty was encountered—neither a teaching assistant nor classmates. Learners frequently wanted to understand the structure of the disc, just as they thumb through a textbook to see how an author assembled it and discover what is important to learn. This is easy to provide, but was not a part of these discs.

Another limitation is the novelty of the hardware for learners. The patience of learners for the "glitches" in hardware and software was clearly less than that of developers. Often the apparent problems were soluble by a sophisticated user, but not by those unfamiliar with the technology.

The gatekeepers (faculty) were somewhat skeptical of the value of the devices. Faculty are not under pressure to educate more efficiently. Although they admired what the technology could do, they rarely saw it as indispensable. They perceived its greatest value to be providing opportunities to "perform" experiments that are too difficult or expensive to conduct with existing college resources.

In conclusion, Davis sees science lab videodiscs as most valuable in the following four situations: when the investigation is time-consuming, when the procedures are potentially dangerous (as when toxic chemicals are involved), when the equipment or materials are expensive, and when it is judged valuable to be able to approximate hypothetical conditions. Given any of these needs, the videodisc is appropriate and useful. But the state of the art in producing videodiscs and the associated software is not very advanced. Many problems of design and production need to be worked out.

Industrial Training

Although there is much more integrated videodisc training in the business and industrial sectors, there has been almost no formal evaluation of the efforts. For industrial sponsors, the bottom line is adequate job performance for a given cost of training. Adequate performance is likely to be assessed informally or in reports that are proprietary. The continued growth in the development of this type of training is evidence of satisfaction among current users. The suppliers claim that, in appropriate situations, this type of training reduces instructional time by 25% and increases retention by 50%. Typical of the reasoning of users is the following excerpt from *Fortune* magazine (Main, 1984):

> J. C. Penney chose interactive training to teach inventory control partly because classes and books on the subject are so boring. 'You can lose half your class,' says Ted Boggio, manager of Penney's merchandise systems training. 'They doze off. Videodisc is dynamic. We can provide talking heads and interesting visuals. We add life, interest, dialogue, spark, into what is really a deadly dull subject.' Penney finds the new course teaches students what they need to know in half the time of the old one. (p. 86)

Smith (1984) performed a controlled comparison of videodisc and classroom training. The course entailed teaching specialists how to determine the eligibility requirements for Aid to Families with Dependent Children. Students in the interactive system, working at their own pace, finished 25% faster—in 120 hours compared with 160 hours for classroom instruction. Using a common exam designed originally for the students in the conventional class, 66% of the videodisc students passed the course compared to 50% of students in the traditional classroom. The videodisc students also preferred this type of instruction to other conventional instruction they had experienced. Although the results are impressive, Smith notes that it is not entirely the medium that is responsible for the good results; it is the programming. If the classroom teacher devoted as much care and attention to instruction as did the designers of the videodisc program, then the comparison might not have been so favorable for videodisc.

Smith reported some problems too, illustrative of the early stages of any new technology. Of the 13 videodisc systems in use for the experiment, 5 were not dependable. When a system is built on tutorial concepts this is too high a failure rate.

Another problem related to integrating students into a larger system of training and placement designed around fixed schedules. In the videodisc training, students complete their training at different times, depending on their abilities and prior knowledge. In this particular project it presented problems for managers who could not predict when new trainees would be available for job placement.

The research done to date suggests that when the topic is appropriate, when tutorial instruction is called for, and when the cost is justified in terms of the number of people to be trained, videodisc instruction can be made at least as effective as live classroom instruction— perhaps even more effective.

Chapter 6 _____

Effective Teaching with Electronic Media

This review of research on the effectiveness of instruction with different media leads to several conclusions. First, human learning is a complex process. Learning a new idea or skill involves attending to the stimulus material, recalling prerequisite information, encoding the material, rehearsing it, correcting misunderstandings, and applying it to new situations. The process of instruction—whether face-to-face or with media—is a complex art, involving the careful selection of various activities to motivate a learner, stimulate recall of prerequisite knowledge, provide new stimulus material, guide the learning process, elicit performance, provide feedback, assess attainment, and enhance retention and transfer. To complicate matters, there is great variability in learners on a number of dimensions that affect how much they will profit from a piece of instruction. These include prior knowledge of the topic, basic cognitive skills for learning the particular type of information or skill, metacognitive skills that control the learning strategies, motivation to acquire the new information or skill, and the context in which the learning takes place. Despite the complex nature of learning and instruction, for many instructional tasks programming designed for various media has been found to be very effective. This is true for the teaching of a great variety of topics. In the cognitive domain, mediated programming has been effective at both motivating learners and providing them with new material that is easily grasped and mastered. It is also true for material at various levels of abstraction—facts, concepts, procedures, and principles. In the affective domain, programming for audio and video has been effective in altering beliefs and attitudes regarding people—for example, racial/ethnic minorities or women—and activities such as the study of science. In the motor domain, mediated instruction has provided useful instruction in a variety of topics ranging from carburetor repair to tennis. Some media are better suited to particular instructional tasks than others. Audio and video can both be used to motivate learners and to provide new content for instruction. They are particularly well-suited for reaching large geographically dispersed audiences through the technologies of broadcast radio and television. Electronic text and graphics, like print text, can carry larger amounts of complex information than audio and video. With the computer as the technology, this medium is better suited than audio and video alone for tutorial activities because of its capability to be interactive. There are reasons, then, for choosing one medium and an associated technology for a particular instructional task; but the reasons are as likely to be economic or managerial as they are unique inherent pedagogical qualities of the medium. The effectiveness of any instructional program, in terms of its impact on learners, rests less on the particular medium chosen, than on the (a) software—the instructional design of the program, (b) the hardware—the means of distribution and the capacity for learner control, (c) learners' prior training and intellectual skills, and (d) a number of contextual factors that influence a learner's response to the potential presented in the software and hardware.

THE ESSENTIALS

Software

The most important determinant of effectiveness is the instructional design of the software. The term *software* includes programs for radio or television, as well as programs of various types for a computer. The burden of instruction is carried in the programming, not the medium. In the late 1960s "Sesame Street" changed dramatically the character of preschool educational television. It did so through an entertain-and-teach formula for programming that involves a creative use of drama, comedy, puppets, music, and pacing, coupled with the careful design of instructional sequences with letters and numbers. In other words, "Sesame Street" exploited the video medium in a way that had not been done previously, but it did so by manipulating the software, not the medium.

Hardware

A second determinant of outcomes is the hardware or technology that delivers the medium. This can affect the outcomes of mediated instruction by what Salomon (1985) calls the *afforded activities*. For example, an audio lecture may be an effective way to present a particular body of knowledge. Broadcast radio can transmit this lecture efficiently to a widely dispersed group of learners. But many of the listeners may not understand all of the lecturer's points the first time through. The hardware or technology of audiotape recording can assist this group of learners by affording them an opportunity to listen to the same lecture more than once, or to those parts of the lecture that were particularly difficult to understand. Similarly with electronic text and graphics—a drill-and-practice program affords a learner the opportunity to be tutored in a particular subject matter; a simulation affords the opportunity to practice applying new information to novel situations.

The quality of the instructional sequence is influenced by the interaction of software and hardware considerations. Software for computers is limited in the sophistication of its diagnostic and remedial branching by the size of random access memory and the speed of the processor. A 32-bit processor with 1 million bytes of random access memory can afford more possibilities to the designer of software (and ultimately to a learner) than an 8-bit processor with 16,000 bytes of memory. Similar points can be made regarding the quality of graphics displays, peripherals, and other kinds of hardware. Technology, then, shapes the software by the learning activities that are made possible.

Learner Characteristics

Learners bring to every instructional situation a set of capabilities for learning. These include prior information about the particular subject and basic intellectual skills to decode and process the new material. These interact in many ways to influence the outcome of encounters with mediated instruction. In general, learners with low ability or with little prior information about a topic, profit from highly structured instruction. Learners with high ability who have prior training in a subject profit more from unstructured presentations in which they can control the presentation and construct meaning out of the material (see chapter 1).

Context and the Learner's Mindware

A fourth factor influencing the outcomes of mediated instruction is the so-called *mindware* that the learner brings to the instructional event. Coined by Salomon (1985), the term *mindware* describes a learner's mental set when encountering what others have designed as instruction. In the past, models of learning from media have been built around a one-way influence model in which the learner is a passive recipient of instruction from programming. Using these models, research has been focused on measuring the average effectiveness of a program on a group of learners, with the implicit assumption that learners are passive vessels waiting to be filled with knowledge. In recent years several studies have suggested that an interactive recipro-cal model is more appropriate. For example, Ksobiech (see chapter 1) demonstrated that learners' perception of the instructional purpose of a video lesson radically affects what they derive from viewing it.

Salomon (1983) conceives this phenomenon in terms of Amount of Invested Mental Effort (AIME). He hypothesizes that the amount of mental effort a learner invests in a learning task depends primarily on two factors: perception of the learning-relevant characteristics of the medium and task, and perception of ability to make something out of the material presented. In a series of studies, he found that television is typically perceived to be mentally less demanding than print mate-rial covering comparable content, and that learners report that they typically invest less mental effort when they watch television than when they read print materials. For this reason, he argues, students of higher ability generate fewer inferences from television material. Salomon was able to manipulate the amount of effort students chose to invest in processing television content by telling them the purpose of their viewing. But the important finding for those who would design media instruction is that learners bring certain expectations to the consumption of such instruction, and these assumptions affect the amount of learning that will occur. In many cases the expectations may be so low that one must question the investment in a program unless there is good reason to believe that the target audience will treat it as instruction.

The associations learners make with media are not always negative when it comes to learning. The Open University in Great Britain creates audio, video, and print materials for each of their courses. They find that lower ability learners more frequently choose to listen to the audio lectures because these learners feel they frequently make mistakes when left to interpret the print materials on their own; they think the lecturer will tell them what they need to know to successfully pass the tests. Indeed, the low ability students who report spending more time listening to the audiotapes of the lectures do better on the tests.

Mindware is affected by many factors, including broad cultural beliefs (e.g., television is for entertainment, computers are for games), expectations established by teachers and peers, and the context in which the mediated instruction is used. However shaped, its influence in moderating the potential of instructional programming is great.

SELECTING A MEDIUM

Does the medium contribute anything unique to instruction? Research on the various symbol systems employed by different media shows that each medium cultivates a different set of skills. As an example, Meringoff (1980) found differences between radio and television in what learners report and infer. She used an identical story in an audio-only version and in a video version. Listening to an audio version of a story resulted in children paying close attention to language—the words describing the appearance and motivations of characters. After listening, children made inferences about likely subsequent behaviors of people in the story by drawing on both the story and on their own personal experiences. When the same story was presented in a video version, children attended to the pictorial presentation and remembered what was visually displayed, missing many subtleties captured in the aural presentation. After viewing, children tended to base their inferences only on the video story, and not on their own experiences. There are many other findings from research on how particular media cultivate different skills in learners; these are reviewed by Clark and Salomon (1985). But the findings, although important, are consistent with a view put forth by Olson and Bruner (1974). By and large, although each medium cultivates different intellectual skills in learners, the knowledge gained from similar programming in different media is the same. In other words, when the question is one of whether a radio or television program of the same material will lead learners to the same knowledge, the answer is likely to be yes. It may be that learners who consistently take their instruction from television instead of radio or print will develop a different set of mental skills. If established by additional research, this would be an important outcome, but not one that would help in the selection of one medium or another for any single instructional task.

On what basis, then, can choices of a medium be made? There are several. There are a few useful distinctions to be made about the capacity of the different media; but by and large, the criteria revolve around issues of cost, efficiency and learner preferences. When the subject matter is aural in nature audio is strongly suggested. Interviews, oral exchanges in meetings and lectures all are effective on audio, especially when the instructional goal is to present new content (e.g., a lecture on a topic or a lecture illustrated with interviews and other elements of human interaction). It is also a good medium to provide raw material that learners can use to practice applying abstract concepts. In a political science course, recorded ward meetings or national political conventions can provide illustrations of concepts such as caucusing, ward politics, and securing consensus. It has also been used to provide drill-and-practice in language instruction and other content areas.

Video can provide the same advantages for the presentation of material, although viewers are frequently intolerant of excessive discourse in video productions. Video is less appropriate than audio if verbal discourse is central to the instructional goal, but it is the medium of choice when visuals are central to the instructional goal. The view through an electron microscope or a structural model of a DNA molecule are better shown with video than described with audio alone. Video is also useful to show social customs in a strange country, although much of the content could be carried by audio, given that most audiences are already familiar with the basic building blocks of social customs—language, dress, and conventions for interacting with people in different roles. When motion and sequence are integral to the instructional goal, video is called for; thus it is especially helpful for instruction in motor skills, because it can provide essential cues for visual discrimination and can provide a model of correct performance. Video productions designed to achieve attitude change have been effective when they have been built on an attitude change model which draws on identification with a role model. The role model in a dramatic sequence, for example, displays visible cues suggesting the desired attitude or behavior toward an object or activity. (Where the aural cues to such attitudes or behavior are stronger, of course, audio alone may be sufficient.)

Electronic text is a medium whose characteristics are fast evolving as the technology changes. There are rapid developments in input and output devices (voice input, digitized audio and video, and high resolution monitors capable of displaying photo-like graphics to mention a few). There are also improvements in memory capacity and in the size and speed of the processor. All of these developments are giving the computer increasing capacity to emulate the best of recorded audio and video. It will not be long before computers will be thought of as all-media devices. But, as implemented in typical systems in the mid 1980s, electronic text and graphics is a particularly strong medium for several instructional tasks. Programming using this medium is well-suited to the presentation of text and graphics in small chunks. With sophisticated graphics it can provide detailed pictures and symbolic material in conjunction with text. It is capable of assessing learner comprehension and providing remedial instruction to correct misunderstandings. Its patience with mistakes of learners makes it an ideal tutor. When used for simulations, it affords the opportunity to develop problem-solving skills associated with applying concepts, procedures, and principles to novel situations.

But whether one should use a particular medium for any of these broad purposes should be based on an assessment of the costs and efficiencies of various alternatives. Audio is a relatively inexpensive medium. Compared to video or electronic text, the costs of program development, production, transmission, and reception are quite small. If face-to-face instruction is expensive and not readily available to certain target audiences, then audio may be the medium of choice. But, if the target audience is not accustomed to getting instruction by audio, and is not likely to invest the effort in learning from audio, another medium may be a better choice.

Video is always more expensive than audio. The costs of good production, as well as the cost of distribution and reception, are higher than audio alone. But given the unique needs of an audience it can be justified. For example, in the 1960s there was national recognition of the problems of culturally disadvantaged children. When they reached school they were noticeably behind their more affluent classmates in academic skills. It was noted that broadcast television and the type of programming it typically carried was of interest to this target group, and this gave rise to support for "Sesame Street." Although it was very costly, it could reach the target audience in ways that more costly face-to-face instruction from parents or preschool teachers did not. Although audio (radio) might have carried some of the same content, it was judged that radio would not reach and hold the attention of this audience.

Computer-based instruction is also expensive, although it needs to be thought of differently than audio and video. The cost of producing and distributing good drill-and-practice software can range from $10,000 to $1 million. But the more complex consideration relates to the hardware and personal support associated with its use. Radio and television utilize standardized devices available to all (radio, tape recorder, television) or to many (videocassette playback unit). But computer-based instruction depends on the availability of a computer of a particular type. At this time in history, computers are distributed so unevenly throughout homes and educational institutions that the real costs of choosing electronic text are hard to estimate, but potentially enormous.

Videodisc coupled with computer-based instruction is definitely a costly form of instruction. For industrial organizations with large geographically dispersed employees the cost of face-to-face training is very high. It warrants experiments with the complex and costly hybrid medium of integrated videodisc. Videodisc has successfully met a number of repetitive training needs for industry. On the other hand, most colleges have not had the same pressure to maximize efficiency with electronic media. The distribution of instructional resources has been such that integrated videodisc is not essential to meeting the goals of instruction. For awhile, then, integrated videodisc may be much more appropriate for industrial than academic settings.

Can the media teach? No, but mediated programming can. With the right software and hardware delivered to receptive students in the proper context, mediated instruction can be very effective for teaching a variety of cognitive and affective topics.

LOOKING BEYOND
MEASURED IMPACT ON LEARNERS

In choosing to develop and use the electronic media for instruction there are several other criteria to consider besides measurable change in viewers' knowledge, attitudes, or behaviors. The potential for having an impact on curriculum and even the character of face-to-face instruction should be considered as well. A number of examples from television make the point (chapter 3). "ThinkAbout" had limited impact on measured problem-solving skills, but it had a very large impact on the school curriculum. Prior to "ThinkAbout" teachers spent virtually no time formally teaching problem-solving skills. When "ThinkAbout" was introduced, teachers began spending 2 hours per week on the topic. This in itself is an impact that can be valued. A similar case can be made for the use of "The Electric Company." In the classrooms where "The Electric Company" was used reading instruction had always been an integral part of the curriculum, but the methods were eclectic. Many teachers were not using the particular skills (e.g., chunking and blending) taught on "The Electric Company"—skills identified by reading experts as important to mastering the skill of reading.

Classroom teachers are generalists, capable of very effective instruction in a wide variety of curricular areas. Once they have completed their pre-service training, most of them do not have the time to master newly developed approaches to a sub-specialty within one instructional domain. Many also find it difficult to maintain a rigorous systematic instructional strategy over an extended period of time (Rosenshine, 1983). Various media can provide both new ideas and day-to-day articulated structure, and do so cost effectively. Whether such an advantage can be exploited, however, depends on the program being acceptable to teachers for this purpose. At a minimum, this requires heavy promotion to gain the attention of teachers. Ultimately, though, it depends on the more basic disposition and skills of teachers in using mediated programming.

A similar argument applies to developing educational television for broadcast to homes. The measured effects of "The Electric Company" in home settings was small, but its daily presence on the air waves set an agenda for home education. It told youth and parents alike that reading is important, and that fundamental decoding skills must be mastered. Similarly, "Sesame Street" continues to be watched in a majority of homes having preschool children. Parents feel comfortable knowing their children are watching the show—whether or not they have evidence that their child has acquired new intellectual skills. In "The Electric Company" evaluation, parents of first graders who viewed the show felt their children had learned reading skills from it. Even if some viewers did not learn all the skills taught, it may have motivated them to be more attentive in the classroom. Direct evidence of this type of effect is not easy to obtain. However, mass communication research has established that frequently watched shows do alter viewers' agenda of what issues are salient and important; there is little reason to think that this phenomenon would not also occur for watchers of educational television.

Electronic media are all around us. Audio, video, and electronic text and graphics are as much a part of daily life as direct experience was a century ago. These media have great potential in the instructional domain, but realizing the potential requires great sensitivity to the many ways it can influence—and be influenced by—those whom we would teach.

References _____

Agency for Instructional Television, Submission to the Joint Dissemination Review Panel, Project TRADE–OFFS. Bloomington, IN: AIT, n.d.

Agency for Instructional Television. *Catalog.* Bloomington, IN: AIT, 1982.

Allen, B. S., Hickey, D., and Molise, G. *Electronic text: An amalgam of capabilities for creating, informing, and instructing.* Monograph No. 2 of the Electronic Text Monograph Series. Washington: Corporation for Public Broadcasting, April, 1985.

Arnheim, R. Virtues and vices of the visual media. In *Media and symbols: The forms of expression, communication, and education,* edited by D. R. Olson for the National Society for the Study of Education, 180–209. Chicago, IL: The University of Chicago Press, 1974.

Ball, S., and Bogatz, G. A. The first year of Sesame Street: An evaluation. Princeton, N.J.: Educational Testing Service, 1970.

Ball, S., and Bogatz, G. A. A summary of the major findings from *Reading with television: An evaluation of The Electric Company.* Princeton, NJ: Educational Testing Service, 1973.

Bangert-Drowns, R. L., Kulik, J. A., and Kulik, C. Effectiveness of computer-based education in secondary schools. *Journal of Computer-Based Instruction* (Summer, 1985), 12:3:59–68.

Bates, A. W. Adult learning from educational television: The Open University experience. In *Learning from television: Psychological and educational research,* edited by M. J. A. Howe. Orlando, FL: Academic Press, 1983.

Beagles-Roos, J. and Gat, I. Specific impact of radio and television on children's story comprehension. *Journal of Educational Psychology* (1983), 75:1:128–137.

Becker, H. J., *School uses of microcomputers: Reports from a national survey.* Issue 1: April, 1983; Issue 2: June, 1983; Issue 3: October, 1983; Issue 4: February, 1984; Issue 5: June, 1984; Issue 6: November, 1984. Baltimore, MD: Center for Social Organization of Schools, The Johns Hopkins University.

Brey, R. and Grigsby, C. *Telecourse student survey 1984*. Austin, TX: The Resources Group, 1984.

Bruce, B. and Rubin, A. How using communication software affects children's writing. Paper presented at the Annual Meeting of the American Educational Research Association, Chicago, April, 1985.

Bryant, J., Alexander, A. F., and Brown, D. Learning from educational television programs. In *Learning from television: Psychological and educational research,* edited by M. J. A. Howe. Orlando, FL: Academic Press, 1983.

Bunderson, C. V. *The TICCIT learner control language* (Occasional Paper No. 5). Provo: Brigham Young University, Institute for Computer Uses in Education, 1975. (ERIC DRS No. ED 158 728).

Burns, P. K. and Bozeman, W. C. Computer-assisted instruction and mathematics achievement: Is there a relationship? *Educational Technology* (1981), 21:10:32-39.

Carroll, J. B. The potentials and limitations of print as a medium of instruction. In *Media and symbols: The forms of expression, communication, and education,* edited by D. R. Olson for the National Society for the Study of Education, 151–79. Chicago, IL: The University of Chicago Press, 1974.

Chu, G. C., and Schramm, W. *Learning from television: What the research says.* 4th edition. Washington, DC: National Association of Educational Broadcasters, 1979.

Clark, R. E. Reconsidering research on learning from media. *Review of Educational Research* (1983), 53:4:445–459.

Clark, R. E. Evidence for confounding in computer-based instruction studies: Analyzing the meta analyses. *Educational Communication and Technology Journal* (1985), 33:4:249–262.

Clark, R. E., and Salomon, G. Media in teaching. In *Handbook of Research on Teaching,* Third edition, edited by M. Wittrock. Chicago: Rand McNally, 1985.

Clements, Douglas H. and Gullo, Dominic F. Effects of computer programming on young children's cognition. *Journal of Educational Psychology* (1984), 76:1051–1058.

Cohen, P. A., Ebeling, B. J., and Kulik, J. A. A meta-analysis of outcome studies of visual-based instruction. *Educational Communication and Technology Journal* (1981), 29:1:26–36.

Cohn, M. R. *Research on the introduction, use, and impact of the ThinkAbout instructional television series, Volume II: Teacher use and student response in three classrooms.* Bloomington, IN: Agency for Instructional Television, 1982.

Constantine, M. Radio in the elementary school. *Science Education* (1964), 48:2:121-132.

Cook, H. R. The effects on learning of structural drills in Spanish broadcast via high frequency AM radio. NDEA Title VII Project No. 1018. Bloomington, IN: Indiana University, 1964.

Cook, T. D., Appleton, H., Connor, R. F., Shaffer, A., Tamkin, G., and Weber, S. J. *"Sesame Street" revisited.* New York, NY: Russell Sage Foundation, 1975.

Corporation for Public Broadcasting. *Research plan for evaluating educational use of technologies.* Washington, DC: Corporation for Public Broadcasting, May 1984.

Dalbey, J., Tourniaire, F., and Linn, M. *Making programming instruction cognitively demanding: An intervention study* (Contract No. NIE 0400830017, from the National Institute of Education, U.S. Department of Education, to the University of California and The Far West Laboratory for Educational Research and Development, (no date).

Davis, B. G. *The evaluation of science lab videodiscs.* Paper presented at the Fifth Annual Nebraska Videodisc Symposium, August, 1984.

DeBloois, M., Maki, K. C., and Hall, A. F. *Effectiveness of interactive videodisc training: A comprehensive review.* Falls Church, VA: Future Systems Inc., 1984.

Edwards, J., Norton, S., Taylor, S., Weiss, M., and Dusseldorp, R. How effective is CAI? A review of the research. *Educational Leadership* (1975), 33:11:147–153.

Elliott, R. W. A study of taped lessons in geography instruction. Westfield, MA: The Abner Gibbs Schools, 1948.

Gagné, R. M. *The conditions of learning.* 3rd edition. New York, NY: Holt, Rinehart and Winston, Inc., 1977.

Gagné, R. M. Learning outcomes and their effects. *American Psychologist* (1984), 39:4:377–85.

Gagné, R. M., and Briggs, L. J. *Principles of instructional design.* New York, NY: Holt, Rinehart and Winston, 1974.

Gay, G. Interaction of learner control and prior understanding in computer-assisted video instruction. *Journal of Educational Psychology* (1986), 78:3:225–227.

Hart-Landsberg, S. *Research on the introduction, use, and impact of the ThinkAbout instructional television series, Volume III: Toward a clear picture of ThinkAbout: An account of classroom use.* Bloomington, IN: Agency for Instructional Television, 1982.

Hartley, S. S. *Meta-analysis of the effects of individually paced instruction in mathematics.* Ph.D. diss., University of Colorado, 1977. Ann Arbor MI: University Microfilms, 1978.

Heron, W. T. and Ziebarth, E. W. A preliminary experimental comparison of radio and classroom lectures. *Speech Monographs* (1946), 13:54–57.

Jamison, D., Suppes, P., and Wells, S. The effectiveness of alternative instructional media: A survey. *Review of Educational Research* (1974), 44:1:1–61.

Johnston, J. Evaluation of curriculum innovations: A product validation approach. In *Improving educational evaluation methods: Impact on policy,* edited by C. Aslanian, 79–100. Beverly Hills, CA: Sage, 1981.

Johnston, J., ed. *New Directions for Program Evaluation, Sourcebook Number 23: Evaluating the new information technologies* (1984, September).

Johnston, J., and Ettema, J. *Positive images: Breaking stereotypes with children's television.* Beverly Hills, CA: Sage, 1982.

Johnston, J., and Ettema, J. Using television to best advantage: Research for prosocial television. In *Perspectives on media effects,* edited by J. B. Bryant, and D. Zillmann. Hillsdale, NJ: Erlbaum, 1986.

Johnston, J., Luker, R., and Mergendoller, J. *Micros in the middle school: A snapshot in 1984.* Bloomington, IN: Agency For Instructional Technology, 1984.

Kozma, R. B. Implications of instructional psychology for the design of educational television. *Educational Change and Technology Journal* (1986), 34:1:11–19.

Ksobiech, K. The importance of perceived task and type of presentation in student response to instructional television. *Audio Visual Communication Review,* 1976, 24:4:401–411.

Kulik, C. and Kulik, J. A. Effectiveness of computer-based education in colleges. *AEDS Journal* (in press).

Kulik, C., Kulik, J. A., and Shwalb, B. J. Effectiveness of computer-based adult education. *Journal of Educational Computing Research* (1986), 2:235–252.

Kulik, J. A., Kulik, C. C., and Cohen, P. A. Research on audio-tutorial instruction: A meta-analysis of comparative studies. *Research in Higher Education* (1979a), 11:4:321–341.

Kulik, J. A., Kulik, C. C., and Cohen, P. A. A meta-analysis of outcome studies of Keller's personalized system of instruction. *American Psychologist* (1979b), 34:4:307–318.

Kulik, J. A., Cohen, P. A., and Ebeling, B. J. Effectiveness of programmed instruction in higher education: A meta-analysis of findings. *Educational Evaluation and Policy Analysis* (1980a), 2:51–64.

Kulik, J. A., Kulik, C. C., and Cohen, P. A. Effectiveness of computer-based college teaching: A meta-analysis of findings. *Review of Educational Research* (1980b), 50:4:525–44.

Kulik, J. A., Bangert, R. L., and Williams, G. W. Effects of computer-based teaching on secondary school students. *Journal of Educational Psychology* (1983a), 75:1:19–26.

Kulik, J. A., and Bangert-Drowns, R. L. Effectiveness of technology in precollege mathematics and science teaching. *Journal of Educational Technology Systems* (1983b), 12:2:137–158.

Kulik, J. A., Kulik, C., and Bangert-Drowns, R. L. Effectiveness of computer-based education in elementary schools. *Computers and Human Behavior* (1985), 1:59–74.

Lepper, M. R. Microcomputers in education: Motivational and social issues. *American Psychologist* (January, 1985).

Lepper, M. R. and Malone, T. W. Intrinsic motivation and instructional effectiveness in computer-based education. In *Aptitude, learning and instruction* edited by R. E. Snow and M. J. Farr (Eds). Hillsdale, NJ: Erlbaum (in press).

Levin, H. M., Glass, G. V., and Meister, G. R. *Cost-effectiveness of four educational interventions,* Project Report No. 84-A11. Stanford, CA: Stanford University, Institute for Research on Educational Finance and Governance, May 1984.

Linn, M. C. The cognitive consequences of programming instruction in classrooms. *Educational Researcher* (May, 1985), 14:5:14–16, 25–29.

Lumley, F. J. Rates of speech in radio speaking. *Quarterly Journal of Speech* (June, 1933).

Main, J. New ways to teach workers what's new. *Fortune,* October 1, 1984:85–94.

Malone, T. W. *What makes things fun to learn? A study of intrinsically motivating computer games.* Palo Alto, CA: Xerox Palo Alto Research Center, 1980.

Menne, J. W., Klingenschmidt, J. E., and Nord, D. L. The feasibility of using taped lectures to replace class attendance. Paper presented at the Annual Meeting of the American Educational Research Association, Los Angeles, March, 1969.

Meringoff, L. K. Influence of the medium on children's story apprehension. *Journal of Educational Psychology* (1980), 72:2:240–249.

Mielke, K. W. and Chen, M. Formative research for *3-2-1 Contact:* Methods and insights. In *Learning from television: Psychological and educational research,* edited by M. J. A. Howe. Orlando, FL: Academic Press, 1983.

NHK Radio-Television Cultural Research Institute. The listening effect of radio English classroom, April 1954–March 1955. Tokyo: NHK, 1956.

Niemic, R. P., Blackwell, M. C. and Walberg, H. J. CAI can be doubly effective. *Phi Delta Kappan,* May, 1986.

Niemic, R. P. and Walberg, H. J. Comparative effects of computer-assisted instruction: A synthesis of reviews. *Journal of Educational Computing Research* (in press).

Office of Technology Assessment. *Informational technology and its impact on American education.* Washington, D.C.: U.S. Government Printing Office, 1982.

Olson, D. R., and Bruner, J. S. Learning through experience and learning through media. In *Media and symbols: The forms of expression, communication, and education: Seventy-third yearbook of the National Society for the Study of Education,*

Part I, edited by D. R. Olson for the National Society for the Study of Education, 125–150. Chicago, IL: The University of Chicago Press, 1974.

Open University of Great Britain. Second submission of the Open University to the Committee on the future of Broadcasting. Milton Keynes, England, April, 1975.

Papert, S. *Mindstorms.* New York, NY: Basic Books, 1980.

Patterson, J. H. and Smith, M. S. The role of computers in higher-order thinking. In *Microcomputers and education: Eighty-fifth yearbook of the National Society for the Study of Education, Part I,* edited by J. A. Culbertson and L. L. Cunningham for the National Society for the Study of Education, 81–108. Chicago, IL: The University of Chicago Press, 1986.

Pea, R. D., and Kurland, D. M. On the cognitive effects of learning computer programming. *New Ideas in Psychology* (1984a), 2:2:137–168.

Pea, R. D., and Kurland, D. M. *On the cognitive prerequisites of learning computer programming* (Technical Report No. 18). New York, NY: Bank Street College of Education, Center for Children and Technology, 1984b.

Perlez, J. Long-distance teaching. *New York Times,* 17 December 1985, p. 19.

Pintrich, P. R., Cross, D., Kozma, R., and McKeachie, W. Instructional psychology. *Annual Review of Psychology* (1985), 37:611–651.

Popham, W. J. Tape recorded lectures in the college classroom—II. *Audio-Visual Communication Review* (1961), 10:94–101.

Rao, P. V. Telephone and instructional communication. In *The social impact of the telephone,* edited by I.D.S. Pool, 473–486. Cambridge, MA: MIT Press, 1977.

Ragosta, M. Computer-assisted instruction and compensatory education: A longitudinal analysis. *Machine-Mediated Learning* (1983), 1:1:97–127.

Reid, A. A. L. Comparing telephone with face-to-face contact. In *The social impact of the telephone,* edited by I.D.S. Pool, 386–414. Cambridge, MA: MIT Press, 1977.

Rice, R. E. *The new media: Communication, research, and technology.* Beverly Hills, CA: Sage Publications, 1984.

Rosenshine, B. Teaching functions in instructional programs. *The Elementary School Journal* (1983), 83:4:335–51.

Rubin, A. and Bruce, B. Quill: Reading and writing with a microcomputer. In *Advances in reading/language research, Volume III,* edited by B. A. Hutson. Greenwich, CN: JAI Press, in press.

Salomon, G. *Interaction of media, cognition and learning.* San Francisco: Jossey-Bass, 1979.

Salomon, G. The differential investment of mental effort in learning from different sources. *Educational Psychologist* (1983), 18:1:42–50.

Salomon, G. Information technologies: What you see is not (always) what you get. *Educational Psychologist* (1985) 20:4:207–216.

Sanders, J. R. *The importance of context when studying the impact of instructional television.* Paper presented at the Annual Meeting of the Evaluation Research Society, Chicago, October, 1983.

Scardamalia, M., and Bereiter, C. Written composition. In *The Handbook of Research on Teaching* (Third edition) edited by M. Wittrock. N.Y.: Macmillan, 1985).

Schramm, W. *Big media, little media.* Beverly Hills, CA: Sage, 1977.

Schmidt, M., Weinstein, T., Niemic, R. P. and Walberg, H. Computer-based instruction with exceptional children: A meta-analysis of research findings. *Journal of Special Education* (in press).

Smith, R. C. *Full-scale pilot testing of Florida's videodisc training project.* Paper presented at the Conference on Interactive Instruction Delivery, Orlando, FL: February 15–17, 1984.

Sunburst. *Sunburst solves your courseware puzzle.* Pleasantville, New York: Sunburst Communications, Inc., 1986.

Vinsonhaler, J. F., and Bass, R. K. A summary of ten major studies on CAI drill and practice. *Educational Technology* (1972), 12:7:29–32.

Williams, D. D., Quinn, W., and Gale, L. E. *Evaluating the use and effect of student-controlled interactive videodiscs.* Paper presented at the annual meeting of the Evaluation Research Society, Chicago, IL: October, 1983.

Wisconsin Research Project in School Broadcasting. Radio in the classroom. Madison, WI: University of Wisconsin Press, 1942.

Wolcott, H. F. *Research on the introduction, use, and impact of the ThinkAbout instructional series, Volume IV: A view of viewers: Observations on the response to and classroom use of ThinkAbout.* Bloomington, IN: Agency for Instructional Television, 1982.

Author Index _____

113

Subject Index _____